THE I

Oswald Chambers' Publications—

APPROVED UNTO GOD
BAFFLED TO FIGHT BETTER
BIBLICAL ETHICS
BIBLICAL PSYCHOLOGY
BRINGING SONS UNTO GLORY
CALLED OF GOD
CHRISTIAN DISCIPLINE, VOLS. 1 and 2
CONFORMED TO HIS IMAGE
DISCIPLES INDEED
GOD'S WORKMANSHIP
HE SHALL GLORIFY ME
IF THOU WILT BE PERFECT
IF YE SHALL ASK
KNOCKING AT GOD'S DOOR
MY UTMOST FOR HIS HIGHEST
NOT KNOWING WHITHER
OUR BRILLIANT HERITAGE
OUR PORTRAIT IN GENESIS
RUN TODAY'S RACE
SHADE OF HIS HAND
SO SEND I YOU
STILL HIGHER FOR THE HIGHEST
STUDIES IN THE SERMON ON THE MOUNT
THE HIGHEST GOOD
THE LOVE OF GOD
THE MORAL FOUNDATIONS OF LIFE
THE PHILOSOPHY OF SIN
THE PLACE OF HELP
THE PSYCHOLOGY OF REDEMPTION
THE SERVANT AS HIS LORD
THE SHADOW OF AN AGONY
WORKMEN OF GOD

OSWALD CHAMBERS: AN UNBRIBED SOUL

THE HIGHEST GOOD

containing also

THE PILGRIM'S SONG BOOK

and

THY GREAT REDEMPTION

by

OSWALD CHAMBERS

OSWALD CHAMBERS PUBLICATIONS
ASSOCIATION
and
MARSHALL, MORGAN & SCOTT
LONDON

MARSHALL, MORGAN & SCOTT
A member of the Pentos group
1 BATH STREET
LONDON EC1V 9QA

THE PILGRIM'S SONG BOOK	1940
THE HIGHEST GOOD	1938
THY GREAT REDEMPTION	1937

This edition (paperback) 1976

ISBN 0 551 05556 I

Printed photolitho in Great Britain by J. W. Arrowsmith Ltd., Bristol
678072L520

CONTENTS

CONTENTS

THE PILGRIM'S SONG BOOK

I

Psalm cxx.

We can judge a nation by its songs. The minor note is indicative of a crushed, but unconquered people. In the Bible there is nothing altogether minor; nothing, that is, of the nature of despair. The Bible deals with terrors and upsets, with people who have got into despair—in fact, the Bible deals with all that the devil can do, and yet all through there is the uncrushable certainty that in the end everything will be all right.

The Songs of Ascents are the autobiography of the children of God; they reveal their inner secrets. These Psalms express not the outward, but the inward condition of the children of God, when they realize that they are pilgrims. We do not immediately realize that we are pilgrims; when a child is born into the world it is welcomed and for a time it feels perfectly happy and at home. Neither when we are born again do we realize at once that we are pilgrims; rather, we feel more at home on the earth than ever; we have come into contact with the Creator of it all, and

> Heaven above is brighter blue,
> Earth around a sweeter green.

But as we go on, this sense of at-home-ness disappears and ultimately we realize a deep alienation to all that the world represents, and we recognize that we are "strangers and pilgrims on the earth", that "here we have no continuing city". That mood is represented in these Psalms. God seems to delight to stir up our nests; it is not the devil who does it, but God; this is curiously unrecognized on our part.

The peace of this world can never be the peace of God. The peace of physical health, of mental healthy-mindedness, of prosperous circumstances, of civilization—not one of these is the peace of God, but the outcome of the souls of men being garrisoned by the prince of this world (see Luke xi. 21). When we are born again from above and realize that we belong to God, we begin to recognize the element of destruction that there is imbedded in many of our Lord's words, e.g., "Think not that I came to cast peace on the earth: I came not to cast peace, but a sword." We realize that the reasoning of the world is not in accordance with the Bible, and we find we are alien to it.

Direction in Distress

"In my distress I cried unto the Lord, and He answered me." (*v.* 1.)

If I am a child of God, distress will lead me to Him for direction. The distress comes not because I have done wrong, it is part of the inevitable result of not being at home in the world, of being in contact with those who reason and live from a different standpoint. We blunder when we try to make out that the prosperity referred to in the Old Testament is intended for us in this dispensation. Plainly that prosperity has never yet been fulfilled in the history of the world; it is going to be fulfilled, but it does not refer to this dispensation, which is the dispensation of the humiliation of the saints, not of their glorification. One of Satan's greatest delusions is to decoy folks off on to blessings that are merely secondary. We become side-tracked if we make physical health our aim and imagine that because we are children of God we shall always be perfectly well; that there will be great manifestations of God's power, thousands saved, etc.

"In my distress . . ." There are elements in our circumstances if we are children of God that can only be described by the word '*distress*'; it would be untruthful to say it was otherwise. "*Then* will I go unto God," says the Psalmist, not "with joy", but "unto God Who is my exceeding joy". We go to God when we have no joy in ourselves and find that His joy is our strength. Are our hearts resting in the certainty that God is full of joy although with us it is 'clouds and darkness' because we are pilgrims?

"I called upon the Lord, and He answered me." It is one thing to cry to God and another thing to hear Him answer. We don't give God time to answer. We come in a great fuss and panic, but when all that is taken out of our hearts and we are silent before God, the quiet certainty comes—'I know God has heard me.'

Deliverance from Deception

"Deliver my soul, O Lord, from lying lips and from a deceitful tongue." (*v.* 2.)

One of the hardest things on earth to bear is deception, especially when it comes through our friends. We do not need the grace of God to stand the deception or slander of an enemy, human pride will stand that; but to be wounded in the house of our friends takes us unawares. Judas had "lying lips"; we read that he "kissed Jesus much". Are we honest with our lips? It is only Christians who can be frank with one another, because their disposition has been altered by God (cf. Ephesians iv. 29).

"What shall be given unto thee, and what shall be done more unto thee, thou deceitful tongue?" (*v.* 3.)

Most of our relationships are carried on with

discreet deceit. The words 'shrewdness', 'diplomacy', 'aye keep a bittie to yersel', express an attitude essential in the life of the world, but a Christian has no time to be a dabster with his tongue, no time to profit by being clever. The teaching of the Sermon on the Mount is never to look for justice but never to cease to give it. We waste our time looking for justice; we have to see that we always give it to others. 'If you are My disciple', Jesus says, 'people won't play you fair; but never mind that, see that you play fair.'

"Sharp arrows of the mighty, with coals of juniper." (*v.* 4.)

The Bible reveals the tongue to be the worst enemy a man has (see James iii. 6–8)—"Sharp arrows of the mighty"—they never miss their mark. The same thing is true when we are born again, God sees that our words get home; but if we are not born again our words rankle and sting and annoy and spread destruction. Sarcasm is the weapon of a weak, spiteful nature, its literal meaning is to tear the flesh from the bone. The antipodes of sarcasm is irony—conveying your meaning by saying the opposite; irony is frequently used by the prophets.

Distraction for a Dwelling

"Woe is me, that I sojourn in Meshech, that I dwell among the tents of Kedar! My soul hath long had her dwelling with him that hateth peace." (*v.* 5.)

Our Lord lived for thirty years in that atmosphere (see John vii. 5). We sing, "There's no place like home," but the author of that song was far away from home when he wrote it. The description the Bible gives of home is that it is a place of discipline. Naturally we do not like what God makes; we prefer our friends to our God-made relations. We are undressed morally in our home life and are apt to be meaner there than anywhere else. If we have been captious and mean with our relations, we will always exhibit that spirit until we become "new creatures in Christ Jesus". That is why it is easier to go somewhere else, much easier often to go as a missionary than to stay at home. God alters the thing that matters.

In a Dilemma by the Disputers

"I am for peace, but when I speak they are for war." (*vv.* 6, 7.)

There is nothing more terrible than for people to take what you say and to turn it into dispute (cf. Psalm cix. 4). We are not to keep things back, but we realize that if we stand for God there will be the dilemma of dispute. "They say: What say they? Let them say." Paul says the same thing—"But with me it is a very small thing that I should be judged of you, or of man's judgment: yea, I judge not mine own self." (1 Corinthians iv. 3.)

In a crisis we are always in danger of standing true to something that is acclaimed by this world rather than standing absolutely loyal to God. Had our Lord been a patriot, He would have been a traitor to His country in submitting to the Roman dominance; He ought to have led an insurrection—'This dominance is wrong, We must break it.' Instead of that, He bowed His head to it. He submitted to the providential order of tyranny knowing that through it God was working out His purposes. "Knowest thou not that I have power to release Thee, and have power to crucify Thee? Jesus answered him, Thou couldest have no power against Me, except it were given thee from above." (John xix 10, 11.)

Note:—No notes are available on Psalm cxxi.

II

Psalm cxxii.

Gladness of Comradeship

"I was glad when they said unto me, Let us go into the house of the Lord." (*v.* 1.)

God begins with us individually in the experience of conscious salvation, then He unites us to one another. Notice the '*altogetherness*' of the saints all through the Epistles—"till we all attain unto the unity of the faith, . . . unto the measure of the stature of the fulness of Christ". None of us individually can reach the "fulness of Christ"; we reach that standard all together. "I have called you friends," said Jesus. The idea is that the presence of Jesus is the arena in which we live. A friend is one who makes me do my best.

Goings of a Community

"Our feet shall stand within thy gates, O Jerusalem." (*v.* 2.)

The gifts of our ascended Lord—"apostles, prophets, evangelists"—are "for the perfecting of the saints". If you should be in advance of the rest of the community, God will take you into 'the ministry of the interior'. Spiritual insight is not for the purpose of making us realize we are better than other people, but in order that our responsibility might be added to. If we neglect to go to God about our communities, our ministers, we become criticizing centres instead of ministers of the interior. God expects us to be intercessors, not dogmatic fault-finders, but vicarious intercessors, until other lives come up to the same standard. Locusts in their flight over a stream may drown by the million, but others keep coming until there is a way for the live ones to go over their bodies. God uses His saints in the same way. "The blood of the martyrs is the seed of the Church." There are prominent names in works of faith, such as Müller and Quarrier, but there are thousands of others whose names are not known. It is the same truth our Lord uttered regarding Himself, "Except a corn of wheat fall into the ground and die, it abideth alone, but if it die it bringeth forth much fruit." The work in a community to begin with may be a wondrous delight, then it seems to die out, and if you do not know the teaching of our Lord you will say it is dead; it is not, it has fallen into the ground and died in its old form, but by and by it will bring forth fruit which will alter the whole landscape.

God's Own City

"Jerusalem is builded as a city that is compact together:" (*v.* 3.)

"For he looked for a city which hath foundations, whose builder and maker is God." (Hebrews xi. 10.)

"And I John saw the holy city, new Jerusalem, coming down from God out of heaven, prepared as a bride adorned for her husband." (Revelation xxi. 2.)

What a curious anomaly—a city of God! We could have understood if it had been the *country* of God, but a holy *city* is inconceivable to us. The city of Jerusalem, like the Temple, was ordained of God, that is why the Children of Israel were so certain the prophets were wrong in saying that God would ever leave Jerusalem; but God did leave it, He left it desolate on account of the sins of the people.

There is a time coming when we shall live in God's own city: Abraham looked for it; John saw it, coming down out of heaven. Our present-day communities are man's attempt at building up the city of God; man is confident that if only God will give him time enough he will build not only a holy city, but a holy community and establish peace on earth, and God is allowing him ample opportunity to try, until he is satisfied that God's way is the only way.

Gathering of the Clans

"whither the tribes go up, the tribes of the Lord, unto the testimony of Israel, to give thanks unto the name of the Lord." (*v.* 4.)

The prophets look forward to the time when all the tribes will meet together in harmony. It is a symbol of what happens in this dispensation of grace; there is absolute harmony in Christ Jesus, no matter what the difference of nationality may be. The Bible is the Charter of the city of God, and all sorts and conditions of people have communion with one another through it. There is a gathering of the clans of all who belong to the race of the twice-born—"Now therefore ye are no more strangers and foreigners, but fellow citizens with the saints, and of the household of God." The saints find their closest unity in communion with God, but we have to be put through a great deal of discipline before the oneness for which Jesus prayed in John xvii. is realized. You will find that God introduces you to teachers and friends who are just beyond you in attainment in order to keep you from stagnation.

Christ's Own Crown

"For there are set thrones of judgment, the thrones of the house of David." (*v.* 5.)

When our Lord stood before Pilate and he asked Him, "Art Thou a King then?" Jesus answered, 'I am a King, but My Kingdom is not of this world, else would My servants fight.' The Kingship of Jesus consists in the entire sanctification of individuals. "For Christ's Crown and Covenant" was the motto of the Scottish Covenanters. Am I eager to be saved and sanctified so that Jesus Christ is crowned King in my life? "Ye call Me Master and Lord: and ye say well; for so I am"—but is He? Is He Lord and Master of our sentiments with regard to this war? of our passions and patriotic pride? We may think He is until we are brought into a crisis, and then we realize that there are whole domains over which He is not Lord and Master. This is true in individual life and in national life.

Generosity of Community

"Pray for the peace of Jerusalem: they shall prosper that love thee." (*v.* 6.)

"Pray for the peace of the city" because it will be better for us as saints if the city is in peace. It is true that in times of war people are driven to God, but the distraction of war upsets the harmony and peace which are essential conditions for the worship of God. Are we set on praying for the peace of Jerusalem only because it will bring prosperity with God to souls?

Goodwill in Concentration

"Peace be within thy walls, and prosperity within thy palaces. For my brethren and companions' sakes, I will now say, Peace be within thee." (*vv.* 7 *and* 8.)

In times of prosperity we are apt to forget God, we imagine it does not matter whether we recognize

Him or not. As long as we are comfortably clothed and fed and looked after, our civilization becomes an elaborate means of ignoring God.

'God bless Jerusalem'—for Jerusalem's sake? No, for my companions' sake. 'God bless the world with peace'—because it is deserving of peace? No, because of the Christians in it. Because God's House is here, we pray 'God bless Askrigg'. Because of the saints in Britain, we pray 'God bless Britain'.

But remember God's blessing may mean God's blasting. If God is going to bless me, He must condemn and blast out of my being what He cannot bless. "Our God is a consuming fire." When we ask God to bless, we sometimes pray terrible havoc upon the things that are not of God. God will shake all that can be shaken, and He is doing it just now.

Graciousness in Compensation

"Because of the house of the Lord our God I will seek thy good." (*v.* 9.)

"Inasmuch as ye have done it unto one of the least of these My brethren, ye have done it unto Me." This is not the judgment of Christians, but of the nations who have never heard of Jesus. They are amazed at the magnanimity of His words—"Lord, when saw we Thee an hungred, and fed Thee?" If that is God's attitude to the nations who do not know Him, what is His attitude toward us? We are never told to walk in the light of conscience, but to walk in the light of the Lord. If Jesus Christ has taught me to be 'as He is in this world', then in every particular in which I am not like Him, I shall be condemned. God engineers circumstances to see what we will do. Will we be the children of our Father in heaven, or will we go back again to the meaner, common-sense attitude? Will we stake all and stand true to Him? "Be thou faithful unto death, and I will give thee a crown of life." The crown of life means I shall see that my Lord has got the victory after all, even in me.

III

Psalm cxxiii.

This Psalm represents the inner biography of faith. It is not easy to have faith in God, and it is not meant to be easy because we have to make character. God will shield us from no requirements of His sons and daughters any more than He shielded His own Son. It is an easy business to sit in an armchair and say, 'Oh yes, I believe God will do this and that'; that is credulity, not faith. But let me say, 'I believe God will supply all my needs', and then let me 'run dry', no money, no outlook, and see whether I will go through the trial of my faith, or sink back and put my trust in something else. It is the trial of our faith that is precious. If we go through the trial, there is so much wealth laid up in our heavenly banking account to draw upon when the next test comes.

Direction of Aspiration

"Unto Thee lift I up mine eyes, O Thou that dwellest in the heavens." (*v.* 1.)

"Unto Thee *lift I up* mine eyes"—we have to make the effort to look up. The things that make it difficult to look up are suffering, or difficulty, or murmuring. If you are suffering, it is intensely difficult to look up. The command to the Children of Israel when they were bitten by the fiery serpent was, '*Look* to the brazen serpent'. We cannot look up if we are murmuring; we are like the child who does not want to do what he is told, and the father comes and says, 'Now look up', but the child won't. We behave like that with God; our circumstances are hard, we are not making progress in life, and the Spirit of God says, 'Look up', but we refuse and say, 'I'm not going to play this game of faith any more'. The counsel given by the writer to the Hebrews is based on the effort of the saint—"*let us lay aside every weight . . .*"; "*let us run with patience the race that is set before us*"; "*looking unto Jesus . . .*"; "*consider Him.*" (ch. xii. 1–3.)

Description of the Attention

"Behold, as the eyes of servants look unto the hand of their masters, and as the eyes of a maiden unto the hand of her mistress; so our eyes wait upon the Lord our God, until that He have mercy upon us." (*v.* 2.)

God intends our attention to be arrested, He does not arrest it for us. The things Jesus tells us to consider are not things that compel our attention"—"Consider the lilies of the field", "Behold the fowls of the air". The Spirit of God instructs us to be attentive. Are our eyes so fixed upon God that we have spiritual discernment and can see His countenance in the dreadful cloud of war? Most of us are at our wits' end, we have no inkling of what God is doing because our eyes have not been waiting upon Him. We are apt to pay more attention to our newspaper than to God's Book, and spiritual leakage begins because we do not make the effort to lift up our eyes to God. "But we all, with open face beholding as in a glass the glory of the Lord, are changed into the same image from glory to glory." (2 Corinthians iii. 18.) That is a description of entire reliance on God. Be careful of anything that is going to deflect your attention from God. It is easier to rely on God in big things than in little things. There is an enormous power in little things to distract our attention from God; that is why our Lord said that "the cares of this world", "the lusts of other things", would choke the word and make it unfruitful.

Distraction of Annoyance

"Have mercy upon us, O Lord, have mercy upon us; for we are exceedingly filled with contempt. Our soul is exceedingly filled with the scorning of those that are at ease, and with the contempt of the proud." (*vv.* 3, 4.)

The thing to heed is not so much damage to our faith in God as damage to our temper of mind. "Therefore take heed to your spirit, that ye deal not treacherously." (Malachi ii. 16.) The temper of mind if it is not right with God is tremendous in its effects, it is the enemy that penetrates right into the soul and distracts us from God. There are certain tempers of mind we never dare indulge in; if we do, we find that they distract us from God, and until we get back into the quiet mood before God our faith in Him is *nil*, and our confidence in human ingenuity the thing that rules.

Spiritual leakage comes not so much through trouble on the outside as through imagining you have 'screwed yourself a bit too high'. For instance, you came to a particular crisis and made a conscientious stand for God and had the witness of the Spirit that everything was all right; but the weeks have gone by, and the months, and you are slowly beginning to come to the conclusion that you had been taking a stand a bit too high. Your friends come and say, 'Now don't be a fool, you are only an ordinary human being; when you talked about this spiritual awakening we knew it was only a passing phase; you can't keep up the strain,

God does not expect you to'; and you say, 'Well, I suppose I was a bit too pretentious.' It sounds wise and sensible, but the danger is that you do not rely on God any longer; reliance on worldly opinion has taken the place of reliance on God. We have to realize that no effort can be too high, because Jesus says we are to be the children of our Father in heaven. It must be my utmost for His highest all the time and every time.

"Have mercy upon us, O Lord, for we are exceedingly filled with contempt." As God's children we have to see that we keep looking in the face of God, otherwise we shall find our souls in the condition of being filled with contempt and annoyance, with the result that we are spiritually distracted instead of spiritually self-possessed. This is true in individual circumstances as well as national crises. It is not always the cross mood that leads to the cross speech, but the cross word that makes the cross mood. If in the morning you begin to talk crossly, before long you will *feel* desperately cross. Take to God the things that perturb your spirit. You notice that certain people are not going on spiritually and you begin to feel perturbed; if the discernment turns you to intercession, it is good; but if it turns to criticism it blocks you in your way to God. God never gives us discernment of what is wrong for us to criticize it, but that we might intercede.

"Unto Thee lift I up mine eyes." The terrible thing is that we are likely to get to the place where we do not miss the consciousness of God's presence; we have gone on so long ignoring the lifting up of our eyes to Him that it has become the habit of our mind and it never bothers us. We go on depending on our own wits and ingenuity until suddenly God brings us to a halt and we realize how we have been losing out. Whenever there is spiritual leakage, remedy it immediately. It does not matter what you are doing, stop instantly when there is the realization that you are losing out before God; lift up your eyes to Him and tell Him you recognize it—'Lord, this thing has been coming in between my spirit and Thee, I am not resting in faith.' Get it readjusted at once. There is always a suitable place to pray, to lift up your eyes to God; there is no need to get to a place of prayer, pray wherever you are. Confess before God that you have been distracted away from faith in Him; don't vindicate yourself. The lust of vindication is a state of mind that destroys the soul's faith in God—'I must explain myself'; 'I must get people to understand'. The remarkable thing about our Lord is that He never explained anything to anybody. Nothing ever distracted Him out of His oneness with God, and He prays "that they may be one, *even as We are one*."

IV

Psalm cxxiv.

Alternative Danger

"If it had not been the Lord who was on our side, now may Israel say;" (*v.* 1.)

Facing an alternative is not to deal in supposition, but part of wisdom and understanding; supposition is wisdom gone to hysteria. In estimating the dangers which beset us we have to remember that they are not haphazard, but things that will happen. Our Lord told His disciples to lay their account with peril, with hatred, in fact He tells them to leap for joy "when men shall hate you, and when they shall separate you from their company, and shall reproach you and cast out your name as evil, for the Son of man's sake". (Luke vi. 22–3.) We are apt to look at this alternative as a supposition, but Jesus says it will happen and must be estimated. It is never wise to under-estimate an enemy. We look upon the enemy of our souls as a conquered foe, so he is, but only to God, not to us.

(*a*) *Estimate of Antagonism.* "if it had not been the Lord who was on our side, when men rose up against us: then they had swallowed us up quick, when their wrath was kindled against us:" (*vv.* 2–3.)

We have to lay our account with the antagonism of men, it is a danger that is always with us. ". . . when *men* rose up against us"—not tendencies, not the moods of men, but men themselves. All that makes life either honourable or terrible is summed up in the word 'men'. In estimating the forces against us we are slow to believe in this antagonistic element, we look at them too haphazardly, not realizing that they are dead set against us. "But beware of men"—it is the last thing we do. The reason our Lord tells us to beware of men is that the human heart is "deceitful above all things, and desperately wicked", and if we put our trust in men we shall go under, because men are just like ourselves, and none of us in our wits before God would ever think of trusting ourselves; if we do it is a sign that we are ignorant of ourselves.

At heart men are antagonistic to the lordship of Jesus Christ. It is not antagonism to creeds or points of view, but antagonism encountered *for My sake.* Many of us awaken antagonism by our way of stating things; we have to distinguish between being persecuted for some notion of our own and being persecuted 'for My sake'. We are apt to think only of the bad things as being against Jesus, but it is the refined things, the cultured things, the religious things which are dead against Jesus Christ unless they are loyal to Him. It was the religious people of our Lord's time who withstood Him, not the worldly. "If the world hate you, ye know that it hated Me before it hated you." (John xv. 18.) These are the deliberate words of our Lord to His disciples. In the measure in which we are loyal to Jesus Christ the same thing happens to us; we are at a loss to understand why people should have the most apparently absurd antipathy to us. Their anger is strangely unaccountable; it is not irritation, but an inspired working against.

(*b*) *Estimate of Agony.* "then the waters had overwhelmed us, the stream had gone over our soul:" (*v.* 4.)

One element in the alternative danger that attends

the saints of God is the agony it produces. It is strange that God should make it that "through the shadow of an agony cometh Redemption"; strange that God's Son should be made perfect through suffering; strange that suffering should be one of the golden pathways for God's children. There are times in personal life when we are brought into an understanding of what Abraham experienced. "Get thee out of thy country . . ." It is not so much that we are misunderstood, but that suffering is brought on others through our being loyal to God, and it produces agony for which there is no relief on the human side, only on God's side. When we pray "Thy Kingdom come" we have to share in the pain of the world being born again; it is a desperate pain. God's servants are, as it were, the birth-throes of the new age. "My little children, of whom I travail in birth again until Christ be formed in you." (Galatians iv. 19.) Many of us receive the Holy Ghost, but immediately the throes begin we misunderstand God's purpose. We have to enter into the travail with Him until the world is born again. The world must be born again just as individuals are.

(*c*) *Estimate of Annihilation.* "then the proud waters had gone over our soul." (*v.* 5.)

The ultimate result of the danger is annihilation, our Lord leaves us in no doubt about that; He always estimated things in the final analysis. Our Lord teaches that the forces against us work for our annihilation, "And ye shall be hated of all men for My name's sake." Nowadays we do not catch the drift of these words. It is not the question of a law of nature at work, but a law of antagonism, everything that is not loyal to Jesus Christ is against us. "And Saul, yet breathing out threatenings and slaughter against the disciples of the Lord . . ." Saul of Tarsus was spending all his educated manhood to annihilate those who were "of the Way". It is that spirit we have to estimate in the danger that besets us if we are true to God.

Appreciated Deliverance

"Blessed be the Lord, who hath not given us as a prey to their teeth." (*v.* 6.)

The reason some of us are so tepid spiritually is that we do not realize that God has done anything for us. Many people are at work for God, not because they appreciate His salvation, but because they think they should be doing something for other people. Our Lord never called anyone to work for Him because they realize a need, but only on the basis that He has done something for them. The only basis on which to work for God is an esteemed appreciation of His deliverance, that is, our personal history with God is so poignant that it constitutes our devotion to Him. God's deliverance makes us His absolute debtors. Have we taken into account what God has done for us? Estimate the alternative danger, and then begin to call on your soul to bless God for His deliverance. ". . . to whom little is forgiven, the same loveth little".

(*a*) *Entire Escape.* "Our soul is escaped as a bird out of the snare of the fowlers: the snare is broken, and we are escaped." (*v.* 7.)

God does not deliver us gradually, but suddenly, it is a perfect deliverance, a complete emancipation. When the deliverance is realized, it is realized altogether, from the crown of your head to the sole of your foot, and your devotion to God is on account of that deliverance. It is a good thing to begin prayer with praising God for His attributes, and for the way those attributes have been brought to bear on our personal salvation. Let your mind soak in the deliverance of God, and then praise Him for them.

(*b*) *Eternal Element.* "Our help is in the name of the Lord who made heaven and earth." (*v.* 8.)

Our help is not in what God has done, but in God Himself. There is a danger of banking our faith and our testimony on our experience, whereas our experience is the gateway to a closer intimacy with God. Our help is in the Name of the One who delivers. The dangers that beset us are real dangers, and if we estimate them we shall appreciate God's deliverance. Why our Lord said that self-pity was of the devil is that self-pity will prevent us appreciating God's deliverance. When we begin to say 'Why has this happened to me?' 'Why does poverty begin to come to me?' 'Why should this difficulty come, this upset?' it means that we are more concerned about getting our own way than in esteeming the marvellous deliverance God has wrought. We read of God's people of old that "They soon forgot His works . . .", and we are in danger of doing the same unless we continually lift up our eyes to God and bless Him for His deliverances.

V

Psalm cxxv.

The Fastnesses of the Godly

"They that trust in the Lord shall be as mount Zion, which cannot be removed, but abideth for ever." (*v.* 1.)

The security of the eternal God is what we are to have confidence in, and the Psalmist likens that security to the mountains, because a mountain is the most stable thing we know. There is nothing so secure as the salvation of God; it is as eternal as the mountains, and it is our trust in God that brings us the conscious realization of this. The one thing Satan tries to shake is our confidence in God. It is not difficult for our confidence to be shaken if we build on our experience; but if we realize that all we experience is but the doorway leading to the knowledge of God, Satan may shake that as much as he likes, but he cannot shake the fact that God remains faithful (see Timothy ii. 13), and we must not cast away our confidence in Him. It is not our trust that keeps us, but the God in whom we trust who keeps us. We are always in danger of trusting in our trust, believing our belief, having faith in our faith. All these things can be shaken; we have to base our faith on those things which cannot be shaken. (Hebrews xii. 27.)

Our consciousness of God is meant to introduce us to God, not to our experience of Him. Jesus said, ". . . no man is able to pluck them out of My Father's hand". (John x. 29.) No power, however mighty, is able to pluck us out of the hand of God, so long as that power is outside us. Our Lord did not say, however, that His sheep had not power to take themselves out. The devil cannot take us out, neither can man; we are absolutely secure from every kind of enemy, saving our own wilfulness. God does not destroy our personal power to disobey Him; if He did, we would become mechanical and uselcss. No power outside, from the devil downward, can take us out of God's hand; so long as we remain faithful, we are as eternally secure as God Himself.

The Frontiers of God

"As the mountains are round about Jerusalem, so the Lord is round about His people from henceforth even for ever." (*v.* 2.)

There are margins beyond which the Spirit of God does not work. Nightingales will not sing outside certain geographical areas, and that is an exact illustration of the frontiers of God. There is a place where God reveals His face, and that place has moral frontiers, not physical. We can blind our minds by perverse thinking; blind our moral life by crooked dealing in business, or by sin. We can never get away from God geographically, but we can get away from Him morally. The writer to the Hebrews mentions the moral frontier, "Let thy conversation be without covetousness; and be content with such things as ye have." (ch. xiii. 5.) Outside that moral frontier, God does not reveal His face. Let me become impatient, let me fix my heart on gain, and I do not see God. If I enthrone anything other than God in my life, God retires and lets the other god do what it can. The majority of us do not enthrone God, we enthrone common-sense. We make our decisions and then ask the real God to bless our god's decision. We say, 'It is common-sense to do this thing', and God leaves us, because we are outside the frontier where He works. "Keep yourself from the love of money, and be content." Think of the imperative haste in our spirit to wish we were somewhere else! That danger is always there, and we have to watch it. When I wish I was somewhere else I am not doing my duty to God where I am. I am wool-gathering, fooling with my own soul; if I am God's child I have no business to be distracted. If I keep myself from covetousness, content with the things I have, I remain within the frontiers of God. If I have the spirit of covetousness in my heart I have no right to say, 'The Lord is my helper'—He is not, He is my destroyer. I have no right to say I am content and yet have a mood that is not contented. If I am ill-tempered, set on some change of circumstances, I find God is not supporting me at all; I have worried myself outside the moral frontier where He works and my soul won't sing; there is no joy in God, no peace in believing. We have to watch that we are not enticed outside the frontier of our own control, just as soldiers have to watch. If they get outside the frontier of their strategy they will probably be killed, and so we have to watch that we are not enticed outside God's frontier. Remember, no man can take us outside, it is our own stupidity that takes us out. When we realize that we have got outside the moral frontier, the only thing to do is to get back again and realize what the Apostle Paul says in Philippians iv. 11–13.

The Faithfulness of Godliness

"For the rod of the wicked shall not rest upon the lot of the righteous; lest the righteous put forth their hands unto iniquity." (*v.* 3.)

The rod means two things—it is used in counting in the sheep, and it is used to destroy the wild beast that suddenly springs out on the sheep (see Psalm xxiii. 4). The man of sin will have his rod, he will do clever tricks, he will put the mark of the beast on every business system that he sanctions, and those who do not have that mark on them can never do business under the regime of the man of sin. Suppose you find that the people who are 'counted in' under the mark of the beast succeed, and you do not succeed, you may be tempted to negotiate the thing and say, 'Well, I don't know, if I did this thing it would save me; I had better just compromise a bit.' We must never do that. "The rod of the wicked shall not rest on the righteous," God says. There is no need to fear, if we keep within the moral frontiers of God we can say boldly, "The Lord is my helper." We do not need to mind how the wicked bluster and say, 'If you don't do this and that, you will starve.' Be faithful, make holiness your aim, holiness in every relationship —money, food, clothes, friendship—then you will see the Lord in all these domains.

The Fitness of Goodness

"Do good, O Lord, unto those that be good, and to them that are upright in their hearts." (*v.* 4.)

Our Lord warned the disciples that they would be put out of the synagogue, and be killed (see John xvi. 2), but He says, 'Don't mind about that, beware only of not doing your duty according to My commandments, because that will destroy both soul and body in hell.' (See Matthew x. 28, Revelation ii. 10.) We are apt to make salvation mean the saving of our skin. The death of our body, the sudden breaking-up of the house of life, may be the salvation of our soul. In times of peace 'honesty may be the best policy', but if we work on the idea that it is better physically and prosperously to be good, that is the wrong motive; the right motive is devotion to God, remaining absolutely true to God, no matter what it costs.

The Futility of Godlessness

"But as for such as turn aside unto their crooked ways, the Lord shall lead them forth with the workers of iniquity." (*v.* 5.)

There is no reference in the Bible to natural law. We talk of certain things as the inevitable result of what a man does: the Bible says, God. The Psalmist says, "the Lord shall lead them forth." God is active in every relationship; it is not natural law or mathematical logic, but God working all through. No man has a fate portioned out to him; a man's disposition makes what people call his fate. The course of deliberately remaining independent of God ends in damnation, by God's direct decree, not as an inevitable happening; and the course of dependence upon God ends in heaven, by God's decree, not by chance. Either course has God behind it. It is the glorious risk of the Christian life. The Apostle Peter gives the warning, "Beware lest, being carried away with the error of the wicked, ye fall from your own stedfastness." (2 Peter iii. 17.) God does not save us from facing the music, or shelter us from any of the requirements of sons and daughters (see 1 John iv. 4). As long as we remain within the moral frontiers of God, watching our hearts lest we give way to ill-content, to covetousness, or self-pity, the things which take us outside God's frontier, then God says, "*I will in no wise fail thee, neither will I in any wise forsake thee.*"

VI

Psalm cxxvi.

The Emotion of Deliverance

"When the Lord turned again the captivity of Zion, we were like them that dream." (*v.* 1.)

Religion is never intellectual, it is always passionate and emotional; but the curious thing is that it is religion that leads to emotion, not emotion to religion. If religion does not make for passion and emotion, it is not the true kind. When you realize that you are saved, that God has forgiven your sins, given you the Holy Spirit, I defy you not to be carried away with emotion. Religion which makes for logic and reason is not religion, but to try to make religion out of emotion is to take a false step. Our Lord bases everything on life as it is, and life is implicit. For instance, you cannot explicitly state what love is, but love is the implicit thing that makes life worth living. You cannot explicitly state what sin is, but sin is the implicit thing that curses life. You cannot explicitly state what death is, all the scientific jargon in the world cannot define death; death is the implicit thing which destroys life as we know it. A child is a good illustration of the implicit, you cannot imagine a child without emotion, always logical, reasonable and well-balanced, he would not be a child but a prig.

Emotion is not simply an overplus of feeling, it is life lived at white-heat, a state of wonder. To lose wonder is to lose the true element of religion. Has the sense of wonder been dying down in your religious life? If so, you need to get back to the Source. If you have lost the fervour of delight in God, tell Him so. The old Divines used to ask God for the grace of trembling, i.e., the sense of wonder. When wonder goes out of natural love, something or someone is to be severely blamed; wonder ought never to go. With a child the element of wonder is always there, a freshness and spontaneity, and the same is true of those who follow Jesus Christ's teaching and become as little children.

People have the idea that Christianity and Stoicism are alike; the writings of the stoics sound so like the teaching of Jesus Christ, but just at the point where they seem most alike, they are most divergent. A stoic overcomes the world by making himself indifferent, by passionlessness; the saint overcomes the world by passionateness, by the passion of his love for Jesus Christ.

The Excitement of Delight

"Then was our mouth filled with laughter, and our tongue with singing: then said they among the heathen, The Lord hath done great things for them." (*v.* 2.)

They were carried completely off their feet with amazement and delight over what God had done (cf. Genesis xvii. 17; Isaiah lx. 5). A man will say, 'I do not doubt that God can forgive sin, that He can give the Holy Spirit and make men holy, but it cannot possibly mean me! When I come before God I remember all my blunders and sins.' When he realizes that it does mean him, then comes this moral hysteria—'It is too good to be true!' With God a thing is never too good to be true; it is too good not to be true.

Ruskin says that early in life he could never see a

hedgerow without emotion, then later on when problems of heart and life were busy with him he saw nothing in Nature; but as soon as the inner turmoil was settled, not only did he get the old joy back, but a redoubled joy. If we have no delight in God it is because we are too far away from the childlike relationship to Him. If there is an internal struggle on, get it put right and you will experience delight in Him.

The Ecstasy of His Doings

"The Lord hath done great things for us; whereof we are glad. Turn again our captivity, O Lord, as the streams in the south." (*vv.* 3–4.)

Whenever God brings His deliverances they are so supernatural that we are staggered with amazement. It is one of the most helpful spiritual exercises to reckon what God has done for us already. When God wanted to make His ancient people realize what manner of God He was, He said, 'Remember the crossing of the Red Sea', and in the New Testament Paul says, 'Remember, it is the God Who raised Jesus from the dead. . . .' These two things are the unit of measurement of God's power. If I want to know what God can do, He is the God Who made a way through the sea; if it is a question of power for my life, the measurement of that is the Resurrection of Jesus.

"Turn again our captivity, O Lord, . . ." I call upon my soul to remember what God has done and it makes me bold to entreat Him to do it again. It is a crime to give way to self-pity, to be weak in God's strength when all this God is ours. We have to "build ourselves up on our most holy faith". Robert Louis Stevenson asked God to forgive him if he had "shown no morning face"; and Dante places in the lowest circles of Hell those who have been gloomy in the summer air.

The Enlightenment of Drudgery

"They that sow in tears shall reap in joy. He that goeth forth and weepeth, bearing precious seed, shall doubtless come again with rejoicing, bringing his sheaves with him." (*vv.* 5–6.)

We make the blunder of wanting to sow and plough and reap all at the same time. We forget what our Lord said, that "one soweth, and another reapeth". "They that sow in tears . . ."—it looks as if the seed were drowned. You can see the seed when it is in the basket, but when it falls into the ground, it disappears (see John xii. 24). The same thing is true with regard to Sunday School work or meetings, it looks as if everything were flung away, you cannot see anything happening; but the seed is there. "They that sow in tears *shall reap in joy*." "Cast thy bread upon the waters: for thou shalt find it after many days. The seed is the word of God, and no word of God is ever fruitless. If I know that the sowing is going to bring forth fruit, I am blessed in the drudgery. Drudgery is never blessed, but drudgery can be enlightened." The Psalmist says, "Thou hast enlarged me in distress"; the enlargement comes through knowing that God is looking after everything. Before, when I came to a difficult bit of the way I was staggered, but now through the affliction and suffering I can put my foot down more firmly (see Romans viii. 35–39).

VII

Psalm cxxvii.

Direction by Countenancing God

"Except the Lord build the house, they labour in vain that build it: except the Lord keep the city, the watchman waketh but in vain." (*v.* 1.)

"For that ye ought to say, If the Lord will, we shall live, and do this, and that" (see James iv. 13–15).

Do I countenance God like that? not have my face towards Him, but my whole person directed by that dominating thought? One of the greatest evidences that we are born again of God is that we perceive the kingdom of God. When I am born from above I countenance God; the arm of the Lord is revealed and I see God as the Architect, as the One Who is doing all things. God is never away off somewhere else; He is always *there.* It is this fact that needs to be taken into consideration. Do I countenance the fact that God is engineering my bodily life and all that I come in contact with? I mention the body because that is the physical case in which our spirit works. If I do not countenance God in that, my faith is jargon. If I enthrone common sense as God, there are great regions of my life in which I do not countenance God.

"Except the Lord build the house . . .", the house of the mind or heart. God is building us for Himself, not for ourselves. Do I realize that my body is the temple of the Holy Ghost, or am I educating myself for myself? If I have an ambition, just where that ambition rules I do not countenance God, I cannot, because my ambition rules and I won't allow God to thwart it. If I do not countenance God in every relationship of my life I shall end in disaster. We get the life of God all at once, but we do not learn to obey all at once; we only learn to obey by the discipline of life.

Distracted Man

"It is vain for you that ye rise up early and so late take rest, and eat the bread of toil: for so He giveth unto His beloved sleep." (*v.* 2.)

This verse describes an amateur providence. We are all amateur providences, until we learn better; we are most impertinent toward God, we tell Him there are certain things we will never allow to happen in other lives, and God comes and says, 'Don't interfere with that life any more.' Are you 'rising up early' and 'sitting up late' to try and unravel difficulties? You cannot do it. It is a great thing to get to the place where you countenance God and know He rules. It is not done by impulse, but by a settled and abiding conviction based on God's truth and the discipline of life. I know that God rules; and He gives me power to perceive His rule. There is no use sitting up late or rising up early, I must do the work that lies before me, and avoid worry as I would the devil. "It is vain for you to rise up early, to sit up late . . ." If I take time from sleep, God's punishment rests on me; or if I take time in sleep when I should be working, He punishes me. Sloth is as bad as being a fussy workman in God's sight. We have no business to be distracted.

I wonder if we have ever considered the Bible implications about sleep? It is not true to say that sleep is simply meant for physical recuperation; surely much less time than God has ordered would have served that purpose. The Revised Version suggests a deeper, profounder ministry for sleep than mere physical recuperation. "For so He giveth unto His beloved *in* sleep" (marg.). The deepest concerns of our souls, whether they be good or bad, are furthered during sleep. It is not merely a physical fact that you go to bed perplexed and wake clear-minded; God has been ministering to you during sleep. Sometimes God cannot get at us until we are asleep. In the Bible there are times when in the deep slumber of the body God has taken the souls of His servants into deeper communion with Himself (e.g. Genesis ii. 21, xv. 12). Often when a problem or perplexity harasses the mind and there seems no solution, after a night's rest you find the solution easy, and the problem has no further perplexity. Think of the security of the saint in sleeping or in waking, "Thou shalt not be afraid for the terror by night, nor for the arrow that flieth by day." Sleep is God's celestial nurse who croons away our consciousness, and God deals with the unconscious life of the soul in places where only He and His angels have charge. As you retire to rest, give your soul and God a time together, and commit your life to God with a conscious peace for the hours of sleep, and deep and profound developments will go on in spirit, soul and body by the kind creating hand of our God.

Disregarded Munificence

"Lo, children are an heritage of the Lord: and the fruit of the womb is his reward. As arrows in the hand of a mighty man, so are the children of youth." (*vv.* 3–4.)

Things go by threes in the Bible: Father, Son and Holy Ghost; God, Church, converts; husband, wife, children. It is God's order, not man's. Whenever one of the three is missing, there is something wrong. If you have a house, the next thing the Bible counsels is hospitality—"given to hospitality" (Romans xii. 13); "pursuing hospitality" (R.V., marg.); give your whole mind to it. "Be not forgetful to entertain strangers: for thereby some have entertained angels unawares." (Hebrews xiii. 2.) That is the way the blessing comes. When we begin to try to economize, God puts dry rot in us instantly. I don't care what line the economy takes, it produces dry rot. When we have the lavish hand, there is munificence at once. "There is that scattereth, and increaseth yet more; and there is that withholdeth more than is meet, but it tendeth only to want." (Proverbs xi. 24.) It is the 'third' element being recognized. Have I got three factors in my thinking, or only two? Is it God and myself? then I am wrong. It is God and myself for God's purposes. Do I want to be saved that I may be right with God, or that God may get His purpose through me?

Delivering Manœuvres

"Happy is the man that hath his quiver full of them: they shall not be ashamed, when they speak with their enemies in the gate." (*v.* 5.)

It is the element of the 'third' that makes a man wealthy. ". . . trained men, born in his house" (Genesis xiv. 14). Have I been able to reproduce my own kind spiritually? If so, in a time of difficulty I will be brought through magnificently victorious; but woe be to the spiritual man who has never produced his own kind, when the difficulties come there is none to assist, he is isolated and lonely. It is the production of the 'third' that returns to you in victory. When we are right with God, Jesus says, "out of you will flow rivers of living water". Immediately you are in difficulties a thousand and one come to assist in prayer; they face the enemy in the gates. That is the great basal truth of the League of Prayer, the clustering together of the children of God. It is those you have been the means of blessing who keep you from the onslaughts of the enemy. We shall be amazed to find how much we are indebted to people we never think about, simply because they were introduced to God through us, and in our difficulties they come to our aid. There is the wire of communication when the manœuvres take place, and we are happily delivered. The kingdoms of this world are founded on strong men, consequently they go. Jesus Christ founds His Kingdom on the weakest link, a Baby. God made His own Son a Babe. We must base our thinking on the rugged facts of life according to God's Book, and not according to the finesse of modern civilization. Let us not be so careful as to how we offend or please human ears, but let us never offend God's ears.

VIII

Psalm cxxviii.

Seemliness of Sanctity

"Blessed is every one that feareth the Lord; that walketh in His ways." (*v.* 1.)

The remarkable thing about fearing God is that when you fear God you fear nothing else, whereas if you do not fear God you fear everything else. "Blessed is every one that feareth the Lord"; the writer to the Hebrews tells us to fear lest haply there should be any promise of God's of which we come short. (iv. 1.) Are we alert enough along this line? ". . . that walketh in His ways". The word *walk* breathes character, it is the symbol for seemly behaviour. John "looked upon Jesus as He walked" —not in a moment of ecstasy and transfiguration but "as He walked, and saith, Behold the Lamb of God!" "Walk worthily," says the Apostle Paul, worthily, that is, towards God, not towards man, because man's standards are not God's. When a man says he is sanctified the charge is often made, and there is no reply to it, 'Remember, you are not perfect'. A saint is required to be perfect towards God. "*Walk before Me*, and be thou perfect"; the standard of judgment is not man's standard, but God's. Our conduct before men will be judged by whether we walk in the seemliness of sanctity before God. That means conduct according to the highest we know, and the striking thing is that the highest we know is God Himself.

"Be ye therefore perfect, even as your Father which is in Heaven is perfect."

There is something in human nature that enables it to go through a big crisis, but we do need help from God to walk worthily the sixty seconds of every minute. Am I behaving myself in God's sight in the seemliness of sanctity to those who are nearest to me? in my letter-writing? in my study? Is the one great lodestar of my life "walking in His ways"? The thing we have to guard against is wanting to be somewhere else. Have I sufficient of the grace of God to behave myself as His child where I am? It is one thing to feel the sufficiency of God in a prayer meeting and in times of delight and excitement, but another thing to realize His sufficiency in whatever setting we may be—in a thunderstorm or on a calm summer day, in a cottage or a College, in an antique shop or on a moor.

Satisfaction in Strenuousness

"For thou shalt eat the labour of thine hands: happy shalt thou be, and it shall be well with thee." (*v.* 2.)

This verse reveals the connection between the natural creation and the regenerated creation. We have to be awake strenuously to the fact that our body is the temple of the Holy Ghost, not only in the spiritual sense, but in the physical sense. When we are born from above we are apt to despise the clay of which we are made. The natural creation and the creation of grace work together, and what we are apt to call the sordid things, labouring with our hands, and eating and drinking, have to be turned into spiritual exercises by obedience, then we shall 'eat and drink, and do all to the glory of God'. There must be a uniting in personal experience of the two creations. It cannot be done all at once, there are whole tracts of life which have to be disciplined. "Your body is the temple of the Holy Ghost," it is the handiwork of God, and it is in these bodies we are to find satisfaction, and that means strenuousness. Every power of mind and heart should go into the strenuousness of turning the natural into the spiritual by obeying the word of God regarding it. If we do not make the natural spiritual, it will become sordid; but when we become spiritual the natural is shot through with the glory of God.

Security of the Saint

"Thy wife shall be as a fruitful vine by the sides of thine house: thy children like olive plants round about thy table. Behold, that thus shall the man be blessed that feareth the Lord." (*vv.* 3 *and* 4.)

To-day people are altogether ignoring the fact that God has anything to do with human relationships. If we get out of any setting of natural life which God has decreed we shall not be blessed. Take the commandment to "honour thy father and mother", and apply it spiritually. I believe that many a life is hindered from entering into sanctification through not being properly related in disposition to father and mother. It is one of the most practical tests. Am I allowing inordinate affection in any relationship? or envy, or jealousy? If so I am certainly not finding blessing, it is getting dried up. I must maintain the spirit and disposition of my Lord and Master in all the ordinary relationships of life, then I shall realize the marvellous security of the saint.

Supremacy of Sincerity

"The Lord shall bless thee out of Zion: and thou shalt see the good of Jerusalem all the days of thy life." (*v.* 5.)

Sincerity means in the straight. Am I straight in my relationship to God and to other people? If I am the Lord says He will bless me. "And thou shalt see the good of Jerusalem all the days of thy life." It is righteous behaviour that brings blessing on others, and the heart of faith sees that God is working things out well.

Surroundings of Sanity

"Yea, thou shalt see thy children's children, and peace upon Israel." (*v.* 6.)

It is in ordinary surroundings and among commonplace things that the blessing of God is to dwell and reveal itself. "Blessed are they that do His commandments, that they may have right to the tree of life, and may enter in through the gates into the city." (Revelation xxii. 14.) Have I entered in through the gates? There is a time when the exceptional has to rule and the 'right arm' has to go, but that is only a phase. Our Lord was brought up so much in ordinary surroundings that the religious people of His day said that He was "a gluttonous man, and a wine-bibber". His life was unassuming in its naturalness. Read the records of the forty days after the Resurrection, they bear the mark of superb sanity. The test is not the success of a revival meeting, that may be questionable, but the success of living in the commonplace things that make life what it is, letting God carry out His purposes as He will.

THE HIGHEST GOOD

SUMMUM BONUM

"In speaking of the Highest Good as the theme of Ethics, Aristotle observes: 'Every art and every kind of inquiry, and likewise every act and purpose, seems to aim at some good; and, since there are many kinds of actions, and many arts and sciences, it follows that there are many ends also. . . . And, if in what we do there be some end which we wish for on its own account, choosing all the others as means to this, this will evidently be the best of all things. And surely from a practical point of view it much more concerns us to know this good; for then, like archers shooting at a definite mark, we shall be more likely to attain what we want.' "—*The Ethic of Jesus*, by Stalker.

All books on Ethics talk about the '*Summum Bonum*,' i.e. the Greatest Good is the Highest End. In practical life we do not begin by thinking, we begin as common-sense beings without thinking; we live first, and do things right and wrong and mixed up anyhow. The first practical thing we have to face in life is duty, and the Bible begins where common sense begins, viz. in the practical domain. We have to get at what Jesus Christ taught was the Highest Good, then we can understand why He did not accept the standard of life that we accept, and why He plays havoc with all our lesser 'goods' until we get to the supreme Good He had in mind.

When we are born again we see things from a totally new perspective and we think we see all, then we go on a bit further, and when we get to the top of that peak there are regions beyond we never dreamed of, and so on. When we have got exhausted with the vistas before us we are prepared to hear Jesus say, "This is life eternal that they should know Thee the only true God" (John xvii. 3).

Evolution is simply a working way of explaining the growth and development of anything. When evolution is made a fetish and taken to mean God, then call it 'bosh';

but evolution in a species, in an idea, in teaching, is exactly what our Lord taught: born of the Spirit and going on "till we all attain . . ., unto the measure of the stature of the fulness of Christ." To understand means we can reconstruct a thing mentally and leave no element out. When we come to try and understand the Highest Good of our Lord, we must take it in His language, and it will take all time and eternity to understand what that Good is. Whether we live for the Highest Good does not depend on our understanding, but on whether we have the life of the Highest Good in us.

(1) The Greatest Good is the Highest End.

(Matthew vii. 4–14; xviii. 8–9; xix. 16; xxv. 46.)

"When Aristotle and the ancient thinkers spoke of the Highest Good, their meaning was, that, in this earthly life of ours, there is for everyone a single supreme attainment, which if missed, will render life a failure, but, if gained, will render it a success." (Stalker.)

The Shorter Catechism states, in answer to the question, "What is man's chief end?" that "Man's chief end is to glorify God and enjoy Him for ever." It is not what man puts into his body or on his body, but what he brings out of his body (cf. Matthew xv. 17–20), and what he brings out of what he puts on his body, viz. his money, that reveals what he considers his chief end. A great many people imagine they have glorified God when they have given two halfpennies for a penny, or have saved a halfpenny. The highest good to them is to keep economic relations right, the highest Good from Jesus Christ's standpoint never dawns on them. The craze to-day is that the highest good is what a man has to live on: feed him, keep his body healthy, and his moral and religious life will be all right. That is the highest good according to the standard of many. As Christians it is more important to know how to live than what to live on. The attitude of the Christian is not, "I'm but a stranger here, heaven is my home," but rather 'I'm *not* a stranger here.' A stranger is exonerated from many things for which God holds us responsible. Jesus asked His Father to treat His disciples not as strangers but as inmates of the world and to keep them from the evil (John xvii. 13). We have to live in the heavenly places while here on earth.

(2) The Greatest Good is the Highest Evangel.

(Matthew iv. 23; ix. 35; xi. 5; xxiv. 14; xxvi. 13.)

In the teaching of Jesus the term 'The Greatest Good' is embodied in its most comprehensive sense in His use of the word 'Gospel.' Our Lord in no way means what we commonly mean when we say 'Gospel,' viz. salvation by faith in Jesus. The Bible never gives definitions, the Bible states facts, and the Gospel that Jesus brought of good news about God is the most astounding thing the world ever heard, but it must be the Gospel that Jesus brought. Whenever the Gospel of Jesus loses the note of unutterable gladness, it is like salt that has lost its savour. We are apt to think of the Gospel on the lines of spring-cleaning. We have conceived of the kingdom of God in the time of the Millennium only, consequently when we come to the parables we are confused. The kingdom of God in this dispensation is the rule of God discerned by individuals alone (see John iii. 3). 'Unless you are born from above,' Jesus says, 'you will never see the rule of God.' It is not seen by the intellect. The rule of God which individual saints see and recognize is 'without observation' in this dispensation. There is another dispensation coming when the whole world will see it as individuals have seen it.

"The kingdom of God is within you" (Luke xvii. 20–3). The blessedness of the gospel of the kingdom of God in this dispensation is that a man is born from above while he is below, and he actually sees with the eyes of his spirit the rule of God in the devil's territory. You will see how far we have got away from Jesus Christ's teaching. We bring in all kinds of things, we talk about salvation and sanctification and forgiveness of sins; Jesus did not mention these things to Nicodemus (He mentioned them later to the disciples), He said, 'Be born from above and you will see the rule of God.' It is an attitude of essential simplicity all through. Preaching what we call the Gospel, i.e. salvation from hell does not appeal to men; but once get Jesus Christ to preach His own Gospel and the Spirit of God to expound it, then men are hauled up at once.

Consideration of Several Beatitudes.

"The drift of the Beatitudes has often been misunderstood. They have been supposed to describe the characteristics of true Christians, pronouncing those blessed who possess such-and-such qualities. But the structure is much more complex. . . . For example, one of the Beatitudes says, 'Blessed are they that mourn': and, if we stop there, the statement is almost equivalent to the absurd saying, 'Happy are the unhappy.' The addition, however, of the words, 'for they shall be comforted,' makes all the difference. . . . And the same principle applies to all the Beatitudes. . . . Thus, mourning, hungering, persecution are not in themselves and by themselves, desirable, but the reverse; yet, taken along with what is given by Jesus to those thus circumstanced, they are blessedness itself." (Stalker.)

"*Blessed are the meek: for they shall inherit the earth.*" The gift here is the heritage of the earth by being fool enough to let other people have it at present. Jesus Christ taught that any one who possesses property of any nature has got to go through a baptism of bereavement in connection with it before he can be His disciple. The rich young ruler is a good specimen of possession (see Luke xviii. 22–3). The craze nowadays for those of us who have no property is to take the liberty of hauling to pieces those who have; but Jesus Christ turns it round the other way—'Do you possess *anything*, any property of pride, any sense of goodness, any virtue, any gift? Then you will have to go through intolerable bereavement before you can ever be My disciple.' Intellectually that is inconceivable; spiritually it is clear to everyone who is rightly related to the Lord. This is where the obstinacy is revealed all through in us as disciples; we come up against this stone wall, and it produces obstinacy. The one great enemy of discipleship to Jesus Christ is spiritual obstinacy, the emphatic 'I won't' which runs all through. Jesus says, 'If you are to be My disciple this and that must go'; we are at liberty to say,

'No, thank you,' and to go away like the rich young ruler with fallen countenances and sorrowful because we have great possessions, we are somebodies, we have opinions of our own, we know exactly what we intend to do.

"Blessed are the merciful: for they shall obtain mercy." As soon as we get right with God we are going to meet things that are contrary, we are going to meet un-merciful good people and un-merciful bad people, un-merciful institutions, un-merciful organizations, and we shall have to go through the discipline of being merciful to the merciless. It is much easier to say, 'I won't bother my head with them'; then we shall never know the blessedness of obtaining God's mercy. Over and over again we will come up against things, and in order to get the eternal blessedness Jesus Christ refers to we shall have to go through the unhappiness of doing something that the standards of men will be contemptuous over.

"Blessed are the pure in heart: for they shall see God." How are we going to be pure in heart? We shall have to go through the humiliation of knowing we are impure. If you want to know what a pure heart is, read the life of the Lord Jesus Christ as recorded in the New Testament. His is a pure heart, anything less is not. Do you know the real panging misery of repentance? Think of the times (they are rare) when you have been in conscious touch with God—the moments when the simplicity of your heart-relationship to God, not your head, was undeterred by a sense of property or possession on your part—that was the time and place to see God.

(3) The Greatest Good is the Healthiest Equity. (Luke vi. 20–3.)

When we try to understand Jesus Christ's teaching with our heads we get into a fog. What Jesus Christ taught is only explainable to the personality of the mind in relation to the personality of Jesus Christ. It is a relationship of life, not of intellect. That is why Jesus said, "Except ye be converted and become as little children, ye shall not enter into the kingdom of heaven." Our conception of things has to be torn to shreds until we realize that what makes a man a Christian is a simple heart-relationship to Jesus Christ, not intellectual conceptions.

This conception enlarges our horizon and enables us to understand why it took God's Son to preach the Gospel, and why Jesus said, "The poor have the gospel preached unto them" (Matthew xi. 5, R.V. marg.). Why not the rich? The rich did not want it. "But if our gospel be hid," says Paul, "it is hid"—from the publicans? No; "it is hid to them that are lost: in whom the god of this world hath blinded the minds of them which believe not." That is the class for whom the Gospel of Jesus has no meaning. A healthy-hided moral man does not want Jesus Christ; a ritualist does not want Jesus Christ; a rationalist does not want Jesus Christ. It is along this line we begin to understand why Jesus said, "I am not come to call the righteous," i.e. the whole and the healthy, "but sinners to repentance." 'I am come to those who mourn, to those who are afflicted, to those who are in a condition of insatiable thirst.' Nothing will ever satisfy a man who is awakened but the supreme Good, viz. the Gospel of God. The social worker who goes into work without this supreme Good ends in heartbreak and disaster because all he succeeds in doing even while he satisfies lesser cravings is to render more intense the craving for something other, viz. the one supreme Good.

"Blessed are ye, when men shall revile you, and persecute you, and shall say all manner of evil against you falsely, for My sake. Rejoice, and be exceeding glad." That is the mark of a Christian from our Lord's standpoint. Many of us are persecuted because we have crochety notions of our own, but the mark of a disciple is suffering "For My sake." Have you ever suffered anything for His sake? If we are foolish enough in the eyes of the world to order our life according to the rule of the kingdom of heaven, the only virtue will be, says Jesus, that men will hate you as they hated Me. Try and work your home life or your business life according to the rule of Jesus Christ and you will find that what He said is true, you will be put out of court as a fool, and we don't like to be thought fools. That is the persecution that many a man and woman has to go through if they are true to Jesus Christ, a continual semi-cultured sneering ridicule; nothing can stand that but absolute devotion to Jesus Christ, a creed will never stand it. Christianity is other-worldliness in the midst of this-worldliness. To apply the rule of the kingdom of God to our daily life is done not by our heads but by the obedience of our hearts. 'If you are ever going to get the true blessedness,' says Jesus, 'it must be by living your life according to the rule of God.' How are we going to discern the rule of God? Jesus told Nicodemus: 'If you are born from above you will *see* the kingdom of God, and *enter into it*' (John iii. 3, 5). Then after we have entered into the kingdom of God, are we going to apply its rule to our bodily life, our mental life, our spiritual life? We are at liberty to stop short at any point, and our Lord will never cast it up at us; but think what we shall feel like when we see Him if all the 'thank you' we gave Him for His unspeakable salvation was an obstinate determination to serve Him in our own way, not His.

RIGHTEOUSNESS

Bear in mind that our human life viewed from a moral standpoint is a tragedy, and that preaching precepts while we ignore the Cross of Jesus Christ is like giving "a pill to cure an earthquake," or a poultice for a cancer. Our attempts to face the problems of human life apart from Jesus Christ are futile. It is good for us to use our common sense and not live tragically, but remember, immediately you touch the moral problem you find that things are damnably wrong, the Book says so; they are so far wrong that it takes the Cross of Jesus Christ to put them right, and we live in a fool's paradise if we ignore the terrific tragedy at the bottom of everything.

"Blessed are they which do hunger and thirst after righteousness: for they shall be filled." (Matthew v. 6.)

"Blessed are they which are persecuted for righteousness' sake: for theirs is the kingdom of heaven." (v. 10.)

"Most people use righteousness as a term for the behaviour of man to man; and it includes this; but, when Christ speaks of hungering and thirsting after righteousness, and of being filled with it, there can be little doubt that, in accordance with the usage of His race, the prize He has in view is the favourable verdict of God on a man's character and conduct." (Stalker.)

The majority of us know nothing whatever about the righteousness that is gifted to us in Jesus Christ, we are still trying to bring human nature up to a pitch it cannot reach because there is something wrong with human nature. The old Puritanism which we are apt to ridicule did the same service for men that Pharisaism did for Saul, and that Roman Catholicism did for Luther; but nowadays we have no 'iron' in us anywhere; we have no idea of righteousness, we do not care whether we are righteous or not. We have not only lost Jesus Christ's idea of righteousness, but we laugh at the Bible idea of righteousness; our god is the conventional righteousness of the society to which we belong.

The claim that our Lord was original is hopelessly wrong, He most emphatically took care not to be; He states that He came to fulfil what was already here but undiscerned. "Think not that I am come to destroy the law, or the prophets: I am come not to destroy, but to fulfil." That is why it is so absurd to put our Lord as a Teacher first, He is not first a Teacher, He is a Saviour first. He did not come to give us a new code of morals: He came to enable us to keep a moral code we had not been able to fulfil. Jesus did not teach new things; He taught "as one having authority"—with power to make men into accordance with what He taught. Jesus Christ came *to make us holy*, not to tell us to be holy: He came to do for us what we could not do for ourselves.

The great tendency to-day is that we are looking for another teacher. The world is sick of teachers and of ideals, the point is, have we ever lived up to any of our ideals? It is not more ideals we want, but the power to live up to what we know we ought to and don't. It is shallowness, not ability, that makes people say we want more teaching and higher ideals—model Sunday School classes, model Bible classes; it is all model. 'Do this and don't do that,' but where is it being carried out? Jesus Christ does not add one burden to the lives of men; He imparts the power to live up to what we know we ought, that is the meaning of His salvation.

"For I say unto you, That except your righteousness shall exceed the righteousness of the scribes and Pharisees, ye shall in no case enter into the kingdom of heaven." (Matthew v. 20.)

"The sympathy of Christ with the training imparted by the Old Testament, and with the passion for righteousness thereby generated, is expressed very distinctly in the Sermon on the Mount, before the Preacher proceeds to the exposition of His own ideal; the motive underlying this declaration being a fear lest His subsequent references to the Old Testament should be understood as disparaging to its authority. In order to avoid this danger, He prefaced His exposition with the statement: 'Think not that I am come to destroy the law or the prophets: I am not come to destroy, but to fulfil.'" (Stalker.)

Jesus Christ contrasts His conception of righteousness with the one already familiar to His hearers. It is not a new gospel we need, that is the jargon of the hour; it is the old gospel put in terms that fit the present-day need, and for one man or one book that does that there are hundreds who tell us that what we want is a new gospel. What we want is men who have the grace of their Lord to face the present-day problems with the old Gospel. What is the good of my talking to the crowd of to-day about the conceptions men had in Luther's day? The thing is, can I make the Gospel I have meet the problems they are facing, and can I show them where other solutions are wrong? If not, I had better keep quiet, I have not been called of God to preach. The majority of us have our own idea of what the Gospel is, but we live aloof from the time we belong to and what we preach is altogether apart from the lives of the folks we talk to.

Our Lord followed the simple line which the prophets took, He took the conceptions He knew men had and compared His own interpretation with theirs and made them judge, with what result? Absolute despair for everybody. Have we ever got hold of the idea that if Jesus Christ was only a Teacher, He was the most tantalizing Teacher that ever came to this earth? If Jesus Christ came to interpret to us a standard infinitely more profound than the one we already have, what is the good of it? He tells us that if we want to see God we must be pure in heart—how are we going to begin? He tells us to love our enemies, to bless them that curse us, to do good to them that hate us, to pray for those who despitefully use us, and persecute us —how can we begin to do it? If He is a Teacher only, then He is a most cruel Teacher, for He puts ideals before us that blanch us white to the lips and lead us to a hell of despair. But if He came to do something else as well as teach—if He came to re-make us on the inside and put within us His own disposition of unsullied holiness, then we can understand why He taught like He did.

It is by facing our lives with the conceptions of Jesus that we understand the meaning of His Cross. One of the most despairing things of our day is the shallow dogmatic competence of the people who tell us they believe in the teachings of Jesus but not in His Atonement. The most unmitigated piece of nonsense human ears ever listened to! Believe in the teachings of Jesus—what is the good of it? What is the good of telling me that I have to be what I know I never can be if I live for a million years—perfect as God is perfect? What is the good of telling me I have to be a child of my Father in heaven and be like Him? We must rid our minds of the idea that is being introduced by the modern trend of things that Jesus Christ came to teach. The world is sick of teachers. Teachers never can do any good unless they can interpret the teaching that is already here.

"For I say unto you, That except your righteousness shall exceed the righteousness of the scribes and Pharisees, ye shall in no case enter into the kingdom of heaven." (Matthew v. 20.)

"Having thus cleared the ground, the Great Teacher proceeds, in the Sermon on the Mount, to expound His conception of righteousness; and, in so doing, He adopts a method frequently resorted to by every expositor who knows his business: He contrasts the conception of the subject in His own mind with one already familiar to His hearers. . . . The righteousness of the scribes was external; that of Jesus is internal. Theirs was a righteousness in words and actions; His flows out from the innermost thoughts and feelings. Theirs was conventional—that is to say, it was intended for the eyes of society; His was a righteousness of the conscience having regard only to God." (Stalker.)

"Except your righteousness shall exceed"—not be different from but '*exceed*,' that is, we have to be all they are and infinitely more! We have to be right in our external behaviour, but we have to be as right, and 'righter,' in our internal behaviour. We have to be right in our words and actions, but we have to be as right in our thoughts and feelings. We have to be right according to the conventions of the society of godly people, but we have also to be right in conscience towards God. Nominal Christians are often without the ordinary moral integrity of the man who does not care a bit about Jesus Christ; not because they are hypocrites, but because we have been taught for generations to think on one aspect only of Jesus Christ's salvation, viz. the revelation that salvation is not merited by us, but is the sheer sovereign act of God's grace in Christ Jesus. A grand marvellous revelation fact, but Jesus says we have got to say 'Thank you' for our salvation, and the 'Thank you' is that our righteousness is to exceed the righteousness of the most moral man on earth.

Jesus not only demands that our external life is above censure but that we are above censure where God sees us. We see the meaning now of saying that Jesus is the most tantalizing Teacher: He demands that we be so pure that God Who sees to the inmost springs of our motives, the inmost dreams of our dreams, sees nothing to censure. We may go on evolving and evolving, but we shall never produce that kind of purity. Then what is the good of teaching it? Listen: "If we walk in the light, as He is in the light, we have fellowship with one another, *and the blood of Jesus Christ His Son cleanseth us from all sin.*" That is the Gospel; Jesus Christ claims that He can take a man or woman who is fouled in the springs of their nature by heredity and make them as pure as He is Himself. That is why He teaches what He does, and it is His standard we are to be judged by if we are His disciples. No wonder the disciples when they heard Jesus speak, said, "Who then can be saved?" The greatest philosophy ever produced does not come within a thousand leagues of the fathomless profundity of our Lord's statements, e.g. "Learn of Me; for I am meek and lowly in heart" (Matthew xi. 29). If Jesus Christ cannot produce a meekness and lowliness of heart like His own, Christianity is nonsense from beginning to end, and His teaching had better be blotted out.

The crucial point of the whole matter is our personal relationship to Jesus Christ. It is far more honest to discard Him absolutely than to play the fool with your own soul and pretend you agree with His teaching while you despise the very central part of it. No wonder Jesus said to a fine godly old man, "Marvel not that I said unto thee, Ye must be born again." If we cannot be made all over again on the inside and indwelt by the Spirit of God, and made according to the teaching of the Sermon on the Mount, then fling your New Testament away, for it will put before you an ideal you cannot reach.

The only way to get out of our smiling complacency about salvation and sanctification is to look at Jesus Christ for two minutes and then read Matthew v. 43–48 and see Who He tells us we are to be like, God Almighty, and every piece of smiling spiritual conceit will be knocked out of us for ever, and the one dominant note of the life will be Jesus Christ first, Jesus Christ second, and Jesus Christ third, and our own whiteness nowhere. Never look to your own whiteness; look to Jesus and get power to live as He wants; look away for one second and all goes wrong.

"When the Son of man cometh, shall He find faith on the earth?" We all have faith in good principles, in good management, in good common sense, but who amongst us has faith in Jesus Christ? Physical courage is grand, moral courage is grander, but the man who trusts Jesus Christ in the face of the terrific problems of life is worth a whole crowd of heroes.

MISSING IT

Anything Jesus Christ revealed may be missed. The disbelief of the human mind always wastes itself in the sentimental idea that God would never let us miss the greatest good. Jesus says He will, that is why we don't like Him, and that is why the teaching of to-day is not the teaching of the Jesus Christ of the New Testament.

(1) What if a Man gain the whole World? (Mark viii. 34–5.)

(*a*) *His Point of View.*

"Whosoever shall come after Me, let him deny himself, and take up his cross, and follow Me. For whosoever will save his life shall lose it; but whosoever shall lose his life for My sake and the gospel's, the same shall save it."

"However the end of life may be conceived—whether as Blessedness, or as the Kingdom of God, or as Righteousness—one thing is indubitable in the entire teaching of Jesus—that He looks upon the end of life as capable of being missed." (Stalker.)

The word translated 'soul' or 'life' may be equally well translated 'himself,' and the verses mean just what they say. Jesus is not defining the great fundamental doctrine of personality, He is talking about the man himself, the person who lives, and with whom we come in contact. Jesus says if a man gains himself, he loses himself; and if he loses himself for His sake, he gains himself.

Bewarc of introducing the idea of time; the instant the Spirit of God touches your spirit, it is manifested in the body. Do not get the idea of a three-storied building with a vague, mysterious, ethereal upper story called spirit, a middle story called soul, and a lower story called body. We are personality, which shows itself in three phases—spirit, soul, and body. Never think that what energizes the spirit takes time before it gets into the soul and body, it shows itself instantly, from the crown of the head to the soles of the feet.

Jesus says that men are capable of missing the supreme good and His point of view is not acceptable to us because we do not believe we are capable of missing it. We are far removed from Jesus Christ's point of view to-day, we take the natural rationalistic line, and His teaching is no good whatever unless we believe the main gist of His gospel, viz. that we have to have something planted into us by supernatural grace. Jesus Christ's point of view is that a man may miss the chief good; we like to believe we will end all right somehow, but Jesus says we won't. If my feet are going in one direction, I cannot advance one step in the opposite direction unless I turn right round.

(*b*) *His Preaching from that Point of View.*

"When He speaks of Blessedness, He at the same time utters woes which will be the portion of some instead of blessedness; when He speaks of the Kingdom, He distinctly thinks of some that will not be able to enter into it; and when He speaks of righteousness, He glances at many who are living in unrighteousness. In short, there is a considerable portion of the words of Christ occupied with the description and denunciation of sin." (Stalker.)

We have, as Christian disciples, to continually recognize that much of what is called Christianity to-day is not the Christianity of the New Testament; it is distinctly different in generation and manifestation. Jesus is not the fountain-head of modern Christianity; He is scarcely thought about. Christian preachers, Sunday School teachers, religious books, all without any apology patronize Jesus Christ and put Him on one side. We have to learn that to stand true to Jesus Christ's point of view means ostracism, the ostracism that was brought on Him; most of us know nothing whatever about it. The modern view looks upon human nature as pathetic: men and women are poor ignorant babes in the wood who have lost themselves. Jesus Christ's view is totally different, He does not look on men and women as babes in the wood, but as sinners who need saving, and the modern mind detests His view. Our Lord's teaching is based on something we violently hate, viz. His doctrine of sin; we do not believe it unless we have had a radical dealing with God on the line of His teaching.

Remember that a disciple is committed to much more than belief in Jesus; he is committed to his Lord's view of the world, of men, of God and of sin. Take stock of your views and compare them with the New Testament, and never get tricked into thinking that the Bible does not mean what it says when it disagrees with you. Disagree with what our Lord says by all means if you like, but never say that the Bible does not mean what it says.

(c) His Procedure and Others'.

"This is the point at which the ethical teaching of Jesus differs most widely from the similar teaching of philosophy. The ethics of the philosophers bear a considerable resemblance to the teaching of Jesus in so far as the setting up of an ideal of character and conduct is concerned; but little or nothing is said by philosophers about the inability of men to attain to the standard, or of the manifold forms of failure exhibited in actual experience." (Stalker.)

People say, 'Oh yes, the Sermon on the Mount is very beautiful, our ideals must be better than we can attain, we shall drift into the Lord's ideals in time somehow or other'; but Jesus says we won't, we will miss them. "The manifold forms of failure exhibited in actual experience" is ignored by other ethical teachers. They say it is never too late to mend—it is; that you can start again—you cannot; that you can make the past as though it had never been—it is impossible; that anyway you can put yourself in such a condition that what you have done need not count—you cannot, and our Lord is the only One who recognizes these things. We think because we fail and forget it, therefore it is overlooked by God—it is not. Jesus Christ's standard remains, and the entrance into His kingdom and into a totally new life is by Regeneration, and in no other way. The teachings and standards of Jesus, which are so distasteful to modern Christianity, are based on what our Lord said to Nicodemus: "Marvel not that I said unto thee, ye must be born again"; otherwise our Lord was a dreamer. The reason we do not see the need to be born from above is that we have a vast capacity for ignoring facts. People talk about the evolution of the race. The writers of to-day seem to be incapable of a profound understanding of history, they write glibly about the way the race is developing, where are their eyes and their reading of human life as it is? We are not evolving and developing in any sense to justify what is known as evolution. We have developed in certain domains but not in all. We are nowhere near the massive, profound intellectual grasp of the men who lived before Christ was born. What brain to-day can come near Plato, or Socrates? And yet people say we are developing and getting better, and we are laying the flattering unction to our souls that we have left Jesus Christ and His ideas twenty centuries behind. No wonder Jesus said that if we stand by Him and take His point of view, men will hate us as they hated Him.

"In spite of his tendency to self-satisfaction, every man is aware some time or other of his own broken bones, and he knows that there must be death before there is any prospect of climbing the heights of moral attainment." (Stalker.)

Have you ever noticed that in some moods you have battled bitterly against the position you know to be right, and all your tirade against it is born of a fear lest after all it might be wrong? That is the real attitude of men and women, they will accept any amount of subterfuges, but right down underneath they have a superb contempt for anything less than that which goes to the root of the matter, and the only One Who does is the Lord Jesus Christ. Sooner or later every human heart flings away as chaff the idea that we are developing and growing better.

(2) What if a Man lose Himself?

(a) The Possibility of the Question.

"For what shall it profit a man, if he gain the whole world, and lose his own soul. Or what shall a man give in exchange for his soul?" (Mark viii. 36–7.)

"Jesus habitually saw with the mind's eye the spiritual development which those around Him might have attained had their desire been fixed more steadily on the true end of life." (Stalker.)

"The idea seems to be, that, even though it does not come to absolute loss, yet if gaining the world involve damage to the self, the moral personality—taint, lowering of the tone, vulgarizing of the soul—we lose much more than we gain." (Bruce.)

In the training of art students, the master does not merely tell them what is wrong in a design, he puts the right design beside the wrong and lets them judge for themselves, and that is exactly what Jesus Christ did all through the Sermon on the Mount.

Do I accept the possibility that I may miss the highest good? There is a sentimental notion that makes us make ourselves out worse than we think we are, because we have a lurking suspicion that if we make ourselves out amazingly bad, someone will say, 'Oh no, you are not as bad as that'; but Jesus says we are worse. Our Lord never trusted any man, "for He knew what was in man"; but He was not a cynic for He had the profoundest confidence in what He could do for every man, consequently He was never in a moral or intellectual panic, as we are, because we will put our confidence in man and in the things that Jesus put no confidence in. Paul says, 'Don't glory in men; don't say, I am of Paul, or I am of Apollos, and don't think of yourself more highly than you ought to think, but think according to the measure of faith, that is, according to what the grace of God has done in you.' Never trust (in the fundamental meaning of the word) any other saving Jesus Christ. That will mean you will never be unkind to anybody on the face of the earth, whether it be a degraded criminal or an upright moral man, because you have learned that the only thing to depend on in a man is what God has done in him. When you come to work for Jesus Christ, always ask yourself, 'Do I believe Jesus Christ can do anything for that case?' Am I as confident in His power as He is in His own? If you deal with people without any faith in Jesus Christ it will crush the very life out of you. If we believe in Jesus Christ, we can face every problem the world holds.

(*b*) *Property and Perdition.*

"Take heed, and beware of covetousness; for a man's life consisteth not in the abundance of the things which he possesseth." (Luke xii. 15.)

"What He thought of most frequently as impeding the growth of true manhood was the pursuit of wealth and property." (Stalker.)

How many people do you know who have their godliness incarnated in economy? Are you one of them? If we can save and do justly with money, we are absolutely certain we are right in the sight of God. The thing about our Lord and His teaching which puts Him immeasurably away from us nowadays is that He is opposed to all possessions, not only of money and property, but any kind of possession. That is the thing that makes Him such a deep-rooted enemy to the modern attitude to things. The two things around which our Lord centred His most scathing teaching were money and marriage, because they are the two things that make men and women devils or saints. Covetousness is the root of all evil, whether it shows itself in money matters or in any way.

(*c*) *Poverty and Perdition.*

"But seek ye first the kingdom of God, and His righteousness; and all these things shall be added unto you." (Matthew vi. 33.)

"But Jesus was hardly less sensible of the danger to which the poor were exposed of missing the prize through an opposite cause—on account, not of the glamour of riches, but the pressure of poverty. . . . His was not a gospel of meat and drink, of loaves and fishes, of better clothes and better houses." (Stalker.)

Jesus Christ nowhere stands with the anti-property league. It is an easy business for me to mentally satirize the man who owns land and money when I don't. It is easy for me to talk about what I could do with a thousand pounds if I had it; the test is what I do with the 2½*d.* I have got. It may be hard for a rich man to enter into the kingdom of heaven, but it is just as hard for a poor man to seek first the kingdom of God. It is not eternal perdition, it is the perdition of losing the soul for this life. Jesus thought as much of the possibility of losing the highest good through poverty as through riches. His own followers were poor, yet He said to them, "Seek ye first"—bread and cheese? money? a new situation? clothing? food? No, "the kingdom of God and His righteousness, and all these things shall be added unto you." Did He know what He was talking about, this poor Carpenter Who had not a pillow of His own and never enough money to pay a night's lodging and yet spoke like that, and Who also said that "the cares of this world, and the deceitfulness of riches, and the lusts of other things entering in, choke the word, and it becometh unfruitful"?

Have I ever tried to practise one thing that Jesus taught in the Sermon on the Mount? Tolstoi blundered in applying the Sermon on the Mount practically without insisting on the need to be born again of the Spirit of God first; but I am taking for granted that we are born again, now try putting into practice something Jesus said, and if what He said does not prove true, say so, but try it. For instance, "Give to him that asketh thee." 'Yes,' you say, 'and be surrounded at once with a crowd of beggars!' Is the Almighty absolutely powerless? We argue like pagans and jargonize like saints. The sentimental jargon in our prayer meetings is exactly like the New Testament language, while in practice we are pagans as if Jesus had never said a word. What man who has never allowed God to lift him up would dare to stand before his fellow creatures and lift up the standard of God? There would be deep condemnation in every message he gave.

Our Lord based a man's self-realization on his spiritual relationship to God. Carlyle estimated human beings by their brains and came to the conclusion that half the human race were fools. Fancy measuring a man by the amount of grey matter in his cranium! You cannot judge a man by his head, but only by his character. One of the greatest disasters in human life is our wrong standards of judgment, we will judge men by their brains, Jesus never did. Jesus judged men and women by their relationship to His Father, an implicit relationship. The brain is nothing more than a marvellous machine for expressing a man's conception of things, and when our hearts and lives are right with God, our brains are a means of expressing a particular conception which comes from our Lord. Never partake of the cynical view of life. Jesus Christ estimates that a man's real soul life is his relationship to God and nothing else, and Paul said, 'Let no man by his philosophy beguile you away from this simplicity'—the simplicity of the life "hid with Christ in God."

IRRESPONSIBILITY

Every Christian worker has to decide this question, viz. Is Jesus Christ's mind infallible, or is the modern Western mind infallible? The tendency abroad to-day is to think ourselves infallible, and the Bible a jumble up of the most extraordinary stuff, good stuff, but we cannot be expected to accept all its views. That means, we believe ourselves more likely to be infallible than Jesus Christ. We would repudiate this statement if made baldly, but we all act as if it were true, we all take for granted that Jesus Christ's teachings are nonsense; we treat them with respect and reverence, but we do not do anything else with them, we do not carry them out.

For the past three hundred years men have been pointing out how similar Jesus Christ's teachings are to other good teachings. We have to remember that Christianity, if it is not a supernatural miracle, is a sham.

(1) This Life's Use Wasted.

"For what shall it profit a man, if he shall gain the whole world, and lose his own soul?" (Mark viii. 36.)

"The most literal meaning of losing one's life is, of course, dying by accident; . . . if a man loses his life by accident, what is the whole world to him?" (*Stalker.*)

Jesus says that life is the opportunity God gives to man to do his life work; that means that God has no respect whatever for our programmes and machinery. Our Lord insists on one thing only, God's purpose for him; He pays not the remotest attention to civilized forces, He estimates nothing but one standard. According to our standards He was idle; for three years He walked about saying things. It is only by putting these violent contrasts before our minds that we understand how different our Lord's standpoint to life is compared with ours. We bend the whole energy of our lives to machinery, and when an accident happens and the machinery breaks up we say, What a disaster. Probably it was the emancipation of the man's life. We make nests here and there, competences here and there, but God has no respect for any of them; at any minute He may send a wind and over goes the whole thing. The one thing God is after is character.

"Not only has the Creator appointed to every human being, in the constitution of his manhood, a certain stature to which he may and ought to attain; but He has appointed a corresponding task for him to fulfil, determined by the providential circumstances in which he is placed. In fact, this is his life; and not to fulfil this God-appointed purpose of his existence is to lose his life." (*Stalker.*)

It is along these fundamental lines that we understand why the Bible says, "There is a way that seemeth right unto a man, but the end thereof are the ways of death"; why Solomon said, "God made man upright; but they have sought out many inventions"; and why he further said, "Trust in the Lord with all thine heart, and lean not upon thine own understanding"; and why our Lord said, "Let not your heart be troubled." The characteristic of a man who is not based on the issue of his life is an incessant cunning, crafty, commercial worry. Our Lord was absolutely devoid of that. What we call responsibility our Lord never had, and what He called responsibility men are without. Men do not care a bit for Jesus Christ's notion of their lives, and Jesus does not care for our notions. There is the antagonism. If we were to estimate ourselves from our Lord's standpoint, very few of us would be considered disciples.

"This idea lay near to the heart of Jesus, first of all, in relation to Himself. He thoroughly realized, from first to last, that He had a work to do, so accurately arranged and fitted to the length of His life that every hour had its own part of the whole to clear off, and He was not allowed either to anticipate or lag behind." (*Stalker.*)

To-day we hold conferences and conventions and give

reports and make our programmes. None of these things were in the life of Jesus, and yet every minute of His life He realized that He was fulfilling the purpose of His Father (e.g. John ix. 4). How did He do it? By maintaining the one relationship, and it is that one relationship He insists on in His disciples, and it is the one we have lost in the rubbish of modern civilization. If we try and live the life Jesus Christ lived, modern civilization will fling us out like waste material; we are no good, we do not add anything to the hard cash of the times we live in, and the sooner we are flung out the better.

In St. John's Gospel this aspect of our Lord's life is more elaborately worked out than anywhere else. It is indicated in the other Gospels (see Luke ii. 49; xiii. 32; xii. 50). Jesus knew He was here for His Father's purpose and He never allowed the cares of civilization to bother Him. He did nothing to add to the wealth of the civilization in which He lived, He earned nothing, modern civilization would not have tolerated Him for two minutes.

"It will be remembered how frequently He represented this life as a trust or stewardship" (*see Luke* xix. 13). *"On one occasion Jesus manifested extraordinary irritation . . . at the sight of a tree that was barren* (*Mark* xi. 12–14); *but this was a manifestation of an impatience, which beset Him always, with objects that were not answering the end of their existence."* (*Stalker.*)

In our Lord's mind any created thing which fails in making anything of its purpose is contemptible. (See Luke xiii. 6–9.) Jesus' attitude to Roman and Grecian civilization was one of superb contempt. Our attitude to Greece and Rome is one of un-bonneted reverence, with not so much as the cast of an eye for Jesus Christ. Our Lord followed life from His Father's standpoint, to-day we are caught up in the shows of things. Take the Bible attitude to men on the whole, civilizations are despatched at a minute's notice, armies come together and annihilate one another and God seems to pay no attention. His attitude is one which makes us blaspheme and say that He does not care an atom for human beings. Jesus Christ says He does, He says He is a Father, and that He, Jesus, is exactly like His Father. The point is that Jesus saw life from God's standpoint, we don't. We won't accept the responsibility of life as God gives it to us, we only accept responsibility as we wish to take it, and the responsibility we wish to take is to save our own skins, make comfortable positions for ourselves and those we are related to, exert ourselves a little to keep ourselves clean and vigorous and upright; but when it comes to following out what Jesus says, His sayings are nothing but jargon. We name the Name of Christ but we are not based on His one issue of life, and Jesus says, "What shall it profit a man, if he shall gain the whole world,"—and he can easily do it—"and lose his own soul?"

(2) This Soul's Way Missed.

"Or what shall a man give in exchange for his soul?" (Mark viii. 37.)

The attitude of our Lord's mind is this, that the eternal condition of a man's spirit is determined by his soul life in this order of things.

"The loss of oneself in missing one's opportunities of moral and spiritual development, . . . may end in the loss of the 'soul' in the awful sense of being cast away for ever. On this solemn subject the teaching of our Lord is extraordinarily copious; indeed, it is to Him that the popular conceptions about a Day of Judgment and the retributions of a future existence are due." (*Stalker.*)

The modern Christian laughs at the idea of a final judgment. That shows how far we can stray away if we imbibe the idea that the modern mind is infallible and not our Lord. To His mind at least the finality of moral decision is reached in this life. There is no aspect of our Lord's mind that the modern mind detests so fundamentally as this one. It does not suit us in any shape or form. The average modern mind reads such passages as Luke xvi. 23–4 and says our Lord was only using figurative language.

If the picture is so dreadful figuratively, what must the reality be like? The things our Lord talks about are either arrant nonsense or they are a revelation of things that the common sense of man can never guess. The attitude of Jesus is outside our standards in every way. We must face the music nowadays as we have never faced it. Christianity is a complete sham or a supernatural miracle from beginning to end; immediately we admit it is a miracle we are responsible for walking in the light of what we know Jesus Christ to be.

To our Lord's mind the definiteness of the finality of punishment was as clear as could be, and nothing but lack of intelligence ever makes us say He did not put it in that way, and if those of us who take Him to be Lord and Master, take Him to mean what He says, where ought we to be in regard to these questions? The majority of us are apologetic about the teachings of Jesus, we are much too easily cowed by modern good taste. The modern mind is the infallible god to the majority of us. A man like Blatchford, who simply puts Jesus Christ on one side, is in a much more wholesome state. It is far better to do that than accept Jesus and leave out what we don't like. That is to be a traitor and a deserter.

The parables in the 25th chapter of St. Matthew are three aspects of the Divine estimate of life. Beware of being an ingenious interpreter. You will always find at the basis of our Lord's parables and illustrations a fundamental consistency to His revelation.

The parable of the ten virgins reveals that it is fatal from our Lord's standpoint to live this life without preparation for the life to come. That is not the exegesis, it is the obvious underlying principle.

The parable of the talents is our Lord's statement with regard to the danger of leaving undone the work of a lifetime.

And the description of the last judgment is the picture of genuine astonishment on the part of both the losers and the gainers of what they had never once thought about.

To be accustomed to our Lord's teaching is not to ask,

'What must I do to be good?' but, 'What must I do to be saved?' How long does it take us to know what the true meaning of our life is? One half second.

Oh, we're sunk enough here, God knows!
  But not quite so sunk that moments,
Sure tho' seldom, are denied us,
  When the spirit's true endowments
Stand out plainly from its false ones,
  And apprise it if pursuing
Or the right way or the wrong way,
  To its triumph or undoing.

There are flashes struck from midnights,
  There are fire-flames noondays kindle,
Whereby piled-up honours perish,
  Whereby swollen ambitions dwindle,
While just this or that poor impulse,
  Which for once had play unstifled,
Seems the sole work of a life-time
  That away the rest have trifled.

There never was anyone who did not have one moment when all the machinery tumbled away and he saw the meaning of his life. God pays not the remotest attention to our civilized cultures and our attitude to things, because that is not what we are here for. We are here for one thing—to glorify God. That is where we join issue with the Lord Jesus Christ to-day, and we look at every other thing as life—"What shall we eat? What shall we drink? Wherewithal shall we be clothed?" Our Lord came for one purpose only, to reveal God, and to get men to be spiritually real.

If we would have the blunt courage of ordinary human beings and face the teachings of Jesus, we would have to come to one of two conclusions—either the conclusion His contemporaries came to, that He was devil-possessed, or else to the conclusion the disciples came to, that He is God Incarnate. Jesus Christ will not water down His teaching to suit our weakness in any shape or form; He will not allow us to cringe in the tiniest degree. Whenever there is a trace of cringing or whining, or wanting something different from what He wants, it is the stern front of the Son of God uncloaking sin every time we look at Him; but if we come as paupers, what happens? Exactly the opposite. He will lift us up and wash us whiter than snow, and put the Holy Ghost in us and place us before the Throne of God, undeserving of censure, by the sheer omnipotence of His Atonement.

What we have to get hold of in our moral lives is that Jesus Christ demands that we live His holy life out naturally. Despair is always the gateway of faith. "If Thou canst!" "All things are possible to him that believeth." So many of us get depressed about ourselves, but when we get to the point where we are not only sick of ourselves, but sick to death, then we shall understand what the Atonement of the Lord Jesus Christ means. It will mean that we come to Him without the slightest pretence, without any hypocrisy, and say, 'Lord, if You can make anything of me, do it,' and He will do it. The Lord can never make a saint out of a good man, He can only make a saint out of three classes of people—the godless man, the weak man, and the sinful man, and no one else, and the marvel of the Gospel of God's grace is that Jesus Christ can make us naturally what He wants us to be.

THE BASE IMPULSE

But, ah, through all men some base impulse runs,
The brute the father, and the men the sons,
Which if one harshly sets himself to subdue,
With fiercer indolence it boils anew,
He ends the worst who with best hopes began,
How hard is this, how like the lot of man!

Experimentally the meaning of life is to attain the excellency of a broken heart, for that alone entails repentance and acceptance, the two great poles of Bible revelation. "The sacrifices of God are a broken spirit"—why, we do not know, but God has made it so. The one thing we are after is to avoid getting broken-hearted.

The base impulse revealed itself in the time of our Lord in three great types of sin—the sin of the publicans, the sin of the Pharisees and the sin of the Sadducees.

"In every country there is a lost class, a class that has given way to the sins of the flesh till its sin can no longer be concealed. What others do by stealth, they do openly. Such a class existed in our Lord's day in Palestine, and the popular names for them in that day were publicans and sinners, or publicans and harlots, or the lost sheep of the house of Israel. . . . The attitude of Jesus to this class was one of the most singular and characteristic features of His career, and, when fully understood, reveals more clearly perhaps than any other circumstance the secret of His mission." (*Stalker.*)

It is remarkable how little Jesus directed His speech against carnal and public sins, though He showed plenty of prophetic indignation against the sins of a wholly different class. He preached His grandest sermon to a bad, ignorant woman (John iv. 10–14), and one of His most prominent disciples was a publican named Matthew. The one man He ever said He wanted to stay with was another publican called Zaccheus, and some of the most fathomless things He said were in connection with a notoriously bad woman (Luke vii. 36–50). It is along this line that we can understand why the Pharisees were sick to the heart and disgusted with Jesus Christ, why they called Him "a friend of publicans and sinners!" We would have done exactly the same to-day in spite of all our religious sentiments. We gloss over our Lord's actions with our civilized conceptions and destroy the meaning of His Gospel.

Our Lord's conduct was not due to any insensibility to the wickedness of open and carnal sins, nor that He was lenient to those sins: He drew near to those sins to make them for ever impossible in the lives of those guilty of them. Jesus roused the conscience of the very worst of them by presenting the highest good. We are apt to forget that our Lord's parables in Luke xv. say just what they do. Never take the fifteenth chapter of St. Luke as an exposition of the Gospel first; it is our Lord's *apologia*; He is explaining to the Pharisees why He is here.

(1) The Pharisaic Invincibility.

In interpreting our Lord's teaching, watch carefully who He is talking to; the parable of the prodigal son was a stinging lash to the Pharisees. We need to be reminded of the presentation of Jesus in the New Testament for the Being pictured to us nowadays would not perturb anybody; but He aroused His whole nation to rage. Read the records of His ministry and see how much blazing indignation there is in it. For thirty years Jesus did nothing, then for three years He stormed every time He went down to Jerusalem. Josephus says He tore through the Temple courts like a madman. We hear nothing about that Jesus Christ to-day. The meek and mild Being pictured to-day makes us lose altogether the meaning of the Cross. We have to find out why Jesus was beside Himself with rage and indignation at the Pharisees and not with those given over to carnal sins. Which state of society is going to stand a ripping and tearing Being like Jesus Christ Who drags to the ground the highest respected pillars of its civilized society, and shows that their respectability and religiosity is built on a much more abominable pride than the harlot's or the publican's? The latter are disgusting and coarse, but these men have the very pride of the devil in their hearts.

Ask yourself, then, what is it that awakens indignation in your heart? Is it the same kind of thing that awakened indignation in Jesus Christ? The thing that awakens indignation in us is the thing that upsets our present state of comfort and society. The thing that made Jesus Christ blaze was pride that defied God and prevented Him from having His right with human hearts. Sin is the independence of human nature which God created turning against God. Holiness is this same independence turning against sin. Sin is not doing wrong things, it is wrong being. Sins are wrong acts: sin is an independence that will not bow its neck to God, that defies God and all He presents, that will not go to the excellency of a broken heart. It is that class who stand for independence in art and culture; it is not for them a question of right or wrong, but of pleasing the senses. The greatest pillars of art and culture are erected on these lines and Jesus Christ pulls down the whole temple, because we cannot build temples of art on this earth at all; they will be built in heaven when the foundations are pure. The refinements of art and culture are all in opposition to the tumbling-in crisis of God in the Incarnation.

(2) The Pride of Integrity.

The conspicuous point of view in which the Pharisees always figure in the Gospels is as incapable of repentance. Self-knowledge is the first condition of repentance. Watch Jesus Christ whenever there is the tiniest sign of repentance, He is the incarnation of forgiving and forgetting, and He says that is God's nature. "I am not come to call the righteous, but sinners to repentance." Remember, that kind of statement hits the Pharisees to the very core of their being. Could they listen patiently to a Man like that? Jesus was killed for His words, He would not have been crucified if He had kept quiet. It was the ruthless way He went straight to the very root of Pharisaism that enraged them until they became the devil incarnate and crucified the Son of God. 'Calvary' means 'the place of a skull,' and that is where our Lord is always crucified, in the culture and intellect of men who will not have self-knowledge given by the light of Jesus Christ.

(3) Sensible Rationalism.

The Sadducee is the type of person who in all ages destroys the treasure of the spirit; he is a common-sense individual.

"There are some people to whom it is never safe to show any valued possession. . . . Now and then someone with the bump of destruction will push his way into our holy of holies, and deface what he considers our idols and leave us sad. . . . Unfold a scheme, a dream, a theory, a long-cherished recollection within the reach of a man who loves destruction, and he will reduce it to nothing. Even a book, that treasure which stands half-way between the tangible and the intangible, is not safe with him, he will turn its pages into ridicule, and give it back with half its charm destroyed."

Thomas Carlyle utterly destroyed the early faith of his wife and never gave her anything in its stead, and Mrs. Carlyle's letters, gifted with the most amazing literary ability and mentality, are wilted and sad, like her face, because he destroyed in the true spirit of the Sadducee her holy of holies and gave her nothing in its place. This line of thought makes us understand our Lord's attitude to the Sadducees, and why He said, 'Don't cast your pearls before swine.' There are some things we must never show to anyone. Like children, we all think that we ought to show our cherished possessions, we ought not; there are Sadducees everywhere. You rarely find them people of uncouth speech, but rather the opposite.

We have all met people who act like an east wind, our mental horizon gets lower and we feel unmitigatedly mean and despicable. When Jesus Christ came near men, He convicted them of sin, but He convicted them also of this, that they could be like He was if they would only come to Him.

"The Sadducees were the anti Pharisaic party, and they went as far in believing too little as the Pharisees in the direction of believing too much. They were the sceptical religious party. Their beliefs lacked warmth and conviction. The weakness of the religious sentiment in them was partly the cause and partly the effect of another characteristic, viz. worldliness. The spiritual and eternal stirred them but faintly, consequently they had a more tenacious hold on the concerns of this present life." (*Stalker.*)

Watch the difference between the faces marred by sin and those marred by coming in contact with the Sadducees, who have all their inner shrines destroyed and nothing given in their place; the latter have a look of withered, mean sanity. Sin does not produce it, it is the effect of the presence of this monster—the rational, healthy-minded Sadducee; this 'monster' has been inside the Christian Church for the past twenty centuries, and is one of the problems that has to be faced. There are comparatively few Pharisees to-day, the greater number are Sadducees, who back up their little bits of common sense against all that Jesus Christ said and against everything anyone says who has had a vision of things differing from common sense.

(4) Sensible Ruling.

"The Sadducees were the ruling class and the priestly party from the date of the Babylonian exile. Such priests have continually emerged in the affairs of God, and they are much more interested in the affairs of the visible world and but faintly tinged with the hope or spirit of the world invisible." (*Stalker.*)

This is the type that perfectly exhibits the Sadducee of our Lord's day. It is not the brutal sceptic who is the Sadducee, he does not destroy anybody's shrines, it is the religious man or woman with particularly bright conceptions of their own, but who are far more concerned with the visible success of this world than with anything else. You go to them with some insurgent doubt in your mind, and they smile at you, and say, 'Oh, don't exercise your mind on those things, it is absurd.' That is the Sadducee who has done more to deface in modern life what Jesus Christ began to do than all the blackguardism and drunkenness in our modern civilization. The subtle destruction of all that stands for the invisible is what is represented by the Sadducee.

It is necessary to get the historical atmosphere and setting of our Lord's life in order to understand the historical exegesis of His teaching. Most of us only know the spiritual exegesis, we come with our spiritual illumination and take incidents out of the Bible—'I don't care about their historic exegesis, I simply take them as expressing my own spiritual condition.' That is not the thing for a student to do; a student has to rightly divide the word of truth, and to find out the historic background of Jesus Christ's teaching.

In Luke xvi. 19–31 we get a good picture of our Lord's attitude to the Sadducees. The rich man *"lived to dine and to wear sumptuous clothing, neither bestowing on the poor any generosity commensurate with his means nor remembering that he was an heir of eternity, and herein is the great moral principle, viz. that of not doing being as guilty as doing, and that the Judge will accept no excuse for a life not marked by unselfishness up to the means of its opportunity."* (*Stalker.*)

If we know that we have received the unmerited favour of God and we do not give unmerited favour to other people, we are damned in that degree. The best and most spiritual people to-day turn Jesus Christ's teaching out of court. They say He could never have meant what He said, and, we have to use common sense. If we apply common sense we run the risk of being Sadducees. What common sense person would carry out the Sermon on the Mount? It is the Sadducee who withers up the true spirit of devotion to God in our life by a 'squirt' of common sense, because the common sense comes from a background of infidelity against God's rule. We are measured by what we do according to what we have. Some people only give to the deserving, because they imagine they deserve all they have. Our Lord says, Give, not because they deserve it, but because I tell you to.

"*Jesus reveals in the parable of the rich man* (*Luke xii.* 16–21) *that his mind and heart have been entirely absorbed with property. About his soul and eternity he has manifested no concern, he heaped up treasure but was not rich towards God.*" (*Stalker.*)

Treasure in heaven is the wealth of character that has been earned by standing true to the faith of Jesus, not to the faith in Jesus. Our Lord's advice to the rich young ruler was, "Sell all that thou hast and give to the poor, and come, follow Me, and thou shalt have treasure in heaven." That is, have faith for the things Jesus Christ stood for, and anybody who is fool enough to conduct his life with Jesus Christ as absolute Master will realize what Jesus said, "Men shall separate you from their company . . . and cast out your name as evil." Many of us are saved by the skin of our teeth, we are comfortably settled for heaven, that is all we care for, now we can make a pile on earth. There are plenty of people who give their testimony all right in meetings, but they are Sadducees to the backbone.

"*The cynicism of the official who feared not God nor regarded man, administered justice in our Lord's instance from mere annoyance. For him justice had no majesty and the misfortune of the widow had no sacredness. That which he could not be got to do, either for the fear of God or out of regard to man, he yet hastened to do merely to save himself from annoyance; and this is a thoroughly Sadducean trait.*" (*Stalker.*) (See Luke xviii. 1–8.)

The spirit of 'I do not wish to be annoyed' is frequently the inspiration of the administration of justice in private cases. It works into our intercession also: I want that bad person saved—because he is of so much value in the sight of God? No, because he is an annoyance to me, I cannot live my life properly with him. That spirit cannot live anywhere near Jesus Christ, because Jesus had only one point of view—His Father's will.

In any work I do for God is my motive loyalty to Jesus,

or do I have to stop and wonder where He comes in? If I work for God because I know it brings me the good opinion of those whose good opinion I wish to have, I am a Sadducee. The one great thing is to maintain a spiritual life which is absolutely true to Jesus Christ and to the faith of Jesus Christ.

THE BASE IMPULSE

Continued

Lord, Lord, when we are dead, remember not
All our lost sorrows and our soul's endeavour,
Better to bear the burden of our lot,
Firmer to stand how strong the storm so-ever,
Only remember all the agony
Thou bearest in the Garden silently.

. . . .

And when the soul by death is freed again,
Thou wilt not let the rapture of her wings
Be marred by memory of this life's pain,
But lift our hearts above our sufferings.
Lord, let our soul's life after all these years
Rise stronger, wiser, cleaner for its tears.

(1) The Low Man with a Little Thing to Do.

The base impulse is the way sin works into our minds and gives us a totally wrong view of God. If the base impulse does not show itself in flesh and blood sins, it will show itself in mean-mindedness. Try and imagine what Jesus meant when He said, "Preach the gospel to every creature"; He keeps 'an open house' for the whole universe. It is a conception impossible of human comprehension.

(*a*) *Moral Distinctions.* We are interested in other men's lives because of a career, a profession, or an ideal we have for them, but God does not seem to care an atom for careers or professions, He comes down with ruthless disregard of all gifts and geniuses and sweeps them on one side; He is interested only in one thing, and that thing was exhibited in the life of our Lord, viz. a balanced holiness before God. Our Lord's character is the full-orbed expression of God's ideal of a man. We can never take any one virtue and say Jesus Christ was the representative of that virtue; we cannot speak of Jesus Christ being a holy Man or a great Man or a good Man; Jesus Christ cannot be summed up in terms of natural virtues, but only in terms of the supernatural. If we can describe a man by any one virtue, he ceases to be God's idea of a man, and the characteristic of the Spirit of God in us is that He brings us "unto the measure of the stature of the fulness of Christ."

(*b*) *Money Matters and the Master's Mind. "Money is the sign and symbol of all earthly possessions; it is earthly pleasure in a solid condition, only requiring to be melted to assume any of its more volatile and usable forms; and the pursuit of it easily becomes an absorbing passion even with those who have forgotten how to turn it into these equivalents. On this subject the language of Jesus is astonishingly severe."* (*Stalker.*)

Jesus saw in money a much more formidable enemy of the Kingdom of God than we are apt to recognize it to be. Money is one of the touchstones of reality. People say, 'We must lay up for a rainy day.' We must, if we do not know God. How many of us are willing to go the length of Jesus Christ's teaching? Ask yourself, how does the advocacy of insurance agree with the Sermon on the Mount, and you will soon see how un-Christian we are in spite of all our Christian jargon. The more we try to reconcile modern principles of economy with the teachings of Jesus, the more we shall have to disregard Jesus. Whenever we read anything that is very plain in our Lord's words, we either say that we cannot understand it or that it has another meaning. Common sense is the best gift we have, but it must be under the dominant rule of God. We enthrone common sense, we do not enthrone God. Men must reason according to their god, and the god of to-day is common sense; that is why Jesus Christ's teaching is ruled out of court. If we try and apply the principles of the Sermon on the Mount to ordinary business life to-day, we shall see where we are. Civilization was founded by a murderer, and the very soul and genius of civilization is competition. What we are trying to do to-day is to Christianize civilization, and our social problems exist because Jesus Christ's teaching is being ruled out.

(2) THE HIGH MAN WITH A GREAT THING TO DO.

"Profound as is His sense of the wickedness of the world and the lostness of the individual, the ground-tone of His preaching is not despair, but hope; and the final and enduring impression left on the mind by the prolonged and sympathetic study of all His words is, that there is an essence of divine dignity and immeasurable value, which it is the task of the Saviour and of all who are inspired with His aims to rescue from the dangers to which it is exposed and to redeem to a destiny of blessedness and immortality." (*Stalker.*)

(*a*) *Solidarity of Sin.* Solidarity means oneness of interest. We are familiar with the phrase 'the solidarity of the human race,' but there is also a solidarity of sin (a oneness of interest in sin), and a solidarity of salvation (a oneness of interest in salvation). I mean by sin, not sin in a particular sense, but in the great big general sense which means a violation or neglect of the laws of morality or religion, and God's Book shows that there is a oneness of interest in all sin. The Psalms show a wonderful discrimination about sin (e.g. Psalms xxxii, li.); they refer to the same thing the Apostle Paul refers to in Ephesians vi. 12, the supernatural inspiration of sin.

We have considered the three great sins of our Lord's day—the sin of the publican, of the Pharisee, and of the Sadducee, and now we must look to the fact that our Lord considered men as evil. "If ye then being evil . . ." (Luke xi. 13). Jesus Christ is made to teach the opposite of this by modern teachers; they make out that He taught the goodness of human nature. Jesus Christ revealed that men were evil, and that He came that He might plant in them the very nature that was in Himself. He cannot, however, begin to do this until a man recognizes himself as Jesus sees him.

We start with the idea that some people are good and some bad; but we are all bad, everyone of us needs saving by Jesus Christ. Imagine that being believed to-day! We can hear Christendom saying, 'Nonsense, human nature is not evil.'

The feature of to-day is the love of man that hates God. We are alienated from the standpoint of Jesus, we have become incarnated by a leaven that never came from His point of view, and if we are going to stand for Him we shall find that what He said is true: "They will turn you out of the synagogues"—not because we denounce sin, a socialist denounces sin as much as a preacher of the Gospel. The difference between a Christian worker and one who does not know Jesus Christ is just this—that a Christian worker can never meet anyone of whom he can despair. If we do despair of anyone, it is because we have never met Jesus Christ ourselves. The social worker who does not know what Jesus Christ came to do will end in absolute despair before long, because the social worker more than anyone else begins to see the enormous havoc that sin has made of human nature, and if he does not know the Saviour from sin, all his efforts will meet with as much success as attempting to empty the Atlantic Ocean with a thimble.

(*b*) *Saviour from Sin.* The great challenge in personal work is—What relationship have I to Jesus Christ? It is not simply that we realize the power of Jesus to save, but that we recognize the possibilities for evil in our own heart, discerned in us by the Holy Spirit, and know that Jesus can save unto the uttermost. Let a man be a murderer, or an evildoer, or any of the things Jesus said men could be, it can never shake our confidence if we have once been face to face with Jesus Christ for ourselves. It is impossible to discourage us because we start from a knowledge of Who Jesus Christ is in our own life. When we see evil and wrong exhibited in other lives, instead of awakening a sickening despair, it awakens a joyful confidence—I know a Saviour who can save even that one. One worker like that is of priceless worth, because through that one life the Son of God is being manifested.

It is not only necessary to have an experience of God's grace, we must have a body of beliefs alive with the Spirit of Jesus, then when we have learned to see men as He sees them, there is no form of disease or anguish or devilishness that can belch up in human life that can disturb our confidence in Him; if it does disturb us, it is because we don't know Him.

The sense of sin is in inverse ratio to its presence, that is, the higher up and the deeper down we are saved, the more pangingly terrible is our conviction of sin. The holiest person is not the one who is not conscious of sin, but the one who is most conscious of what sin is. The one who talked most about sin was our Lord Jesus Christ. We are apt to run off with the idea that a man in order to be saved from sin must have lived a vile life himself; but the One who has an understanding of the awful horror of sin is the spotlessly holy Christ, Who "knew no sin." The lower down we get into the experience of sin, the less conviction of sin we have. When we are regenerated and lifted into the light, we begin to know what sin means. There is no mention of sin in the Apostle Paul's apprehension by Christ, yet no one wrote more about sin than the Apostle Paul years after in his Epistles, because by the marvellous working of God's grace and his own repentance, he was lifted into the heavenly places where he saw what sin really was. The danger with those of us who have experienced God's perfect salvation is that we talk blatant jargon about an experience instead of banking on the tremendous revelation of God the Holy Ghost. The purer we are through God's sovereign grace, the more terribly poignant is our sense of sin. It is perilous to say, 'I have nothing to do with sin now'; you are the only kind of person who can know what sin is. Men living in sin don't know anything about it. Sin destroys the capacity of knowing what sin is. It is when we have been delivered from sin that we begin to realize by the pure light of the Holy Ghost what sin is. We shall find over and over again that God will send us shuddering to our knees every time we realize what sin is, and instead of it increasing hardness in us towards the men and women who are living in sin, the Spirit of God will use it as a means of bringing us to the dust before Him in vicarious intercession that God will save them as He has saved us. Beware of the metallic, hard, un-Christlike stamp of some testimonies to sanctification, they are not stamped by the Holy Ghost. The testimony to sanctification that is of God is dipped and saturated in the blood of the Son of God, and that blood sprang from the broken heart of God on account of sin. When once the soul realizes what sanctification is, it is a joy unspeakable, but it is a joy in which there is the tremendous undercurrent of a chastening humiliation. Beware of any experience that is not built absolutely on the atoning merit of Jesus Christ; and remember, the measure of your freedom from sin is the measure of your sense of what sin is.

THY GREAT REDEMPTION

FOREWORD

Writing in the War years (1917) Oswald Chambers said, 'Through this war there will emerge new re-statements of God and of Christ. To me there emerge two or three grand facts: First, Fathomless Redemption as the basis of human life; absolute God-like Forgiveness of Sin; with a liberty to reject that basis on the part of man. Second, That God's Name is Jesus Christ; not that He is a revelation from God, but that He is God. That means that God became the weakest thing in His creation—a Babe. Third, That He can introduce into any man the heredity of the Son of God by New Birth, in which His Nature becomes operative in human nature, along with a series of educational developments.' These articles on Redemption contribute to that very end. 'Everything that has been touched by sin and the devil has been redeemed; we are to live in the world immovably banked on that faith.' What sure ground for our feet we have in that glorious truth as we stand for Jesus Christ, witnesses unto Him. But the in-working of Redemption in personal life is grandly brought out in these living messages. I quote another sentence, 'Immediately I accept the Cross of Christ as the revelation of Redemption I am not, I must not be, the same man; I must be another man, and I must take up my cross for my Lord.' So we see Redemption working inwardly, with our reactions to it, and with the resultant issues regarding sin and righteousness and judgment. The book is *more* than worth its weight in gold.

DAVID LAMBERT

REDEMPTION

(1) Redemption in Realized Revelation. *John* xix. 30.

We can never expound the Redemption, but we must have strong unshaken faith in it so that we are not swept off our feet by actual things. That the devil and man are allowed to do as they like is a mere episode in the providence of God. Everything that has been touched by sin and the devil has been redeemed; we are to live in the world immovably banked in that faith. Unless we have faith in the Redemption, all our activities are fussy impertinences which tell God He is doing nothing. We destroy our souls serving Jesus Christ, instead of abiding in Him. Jesus Christ is not working out the Redemption, it is complete; we are working it out, and beginning to realize it by obedience. Our practical life is to be moulded by our belief in the Redemption, and our declared message will be in accordance with our belief. If we say we believe "It is finished" we must not blaspheme God by unbelief in any domain of our practical life.

We must make a distinction in our minds between the revelation of Redemption and conscious participation in it. When we are born again we consciously enter into participation of the Redemption. We do not help God to redeem the world: we realize that God has redeemed it. Redemption is not dependent on our experience of it. The human race is redeemed; we have to be so faithful to God that through us may come the awakening of those who have not yet realized that they are redeemed.

(2) Revelation and Redemption in Relation. 2 *Cor.* v. 18–21.

A sinner knows what the Redemption has wrought in him, but it is only long afterwards that he begins to grasp the revelation of how that Redemption was made particularly and in detail possible in him. It is one thing to be saved by God's grace, but another thing to have a clear revelation as to how God did it. Our Lord Jesus Christ is the Revelation complete; the Bible is the revelation come down to the shores of our life in words. The grace of God can never alter; Redemption can never alter; and the evidence that we are experiencing the grace of God in Redemption is that it is manifestly working out in us in actual ways. When the words of the Bible come home to us by the Holy Spirit, the supernatural essence of the Redemption is in those words and they bring forth new life in us. If you have been saved from sin, say so; if you have been sanctified by God's grace, say so. Don't substitute some other refinement in its place. By using other words you are not testifying to God, but compromising with the atmosphere of those to whom you are talking.

The religion of Jesus Christ is not a religion of ethical truth, but of Redemption. The teachings of Jesus have not made so much difference to the world as the teachings of Socrates and Plato, but to those who are born from above they make all the difference. The thing that tells is not that the actual life is lived rightly, but that the motive underneath is right. The characteristic of the Redemption when it works out subjectively in accordance with Scripture is that act of devotion of Mary of Bethany. It was not useful, nor was it her duty; it was an extravagant waste, but the motive of it was the spontaneous originality which sprang from a personal passionate devotion to Jesus Christ. When a man has been profoundly moved in his spirit by the experience of Redemption, then out of him flow rivers of living water. Stop the concern of whether you are of any use in the world. "He that believeth in me," said Jesus, "out of him shall flow rivers of living water"; whether we see it or not is a matter of indifference. Heed the Source.

(3) REDEMPTION IN OBJECTIVE FORM. *Luke* xxiv. 44–7.

The disciples after the Resurrection received into themselves an influx from the risen Christ—"their eyes were opened, and they knew Him" (*v.* 31); and their minds were opened, "that they might understand the Scriptures" (*v.* 45). The characteristic of being born again is that we know Who Jesus is. The secret of the Christian is that he knows the absolute Deity of the Lord Jesus Christ. When we are saved by God's grace our minds are opened by the incoming of the Holy Spirit and we understand the Scriptures. The test of regeneration is that the Bible instantly becomes the Book of books to us.

The objective form of the Redemption comes to us through the Person of the Lord Jesus Christ, and works itself out in saving judgments. The bedrock of Christianity is repentance. There is a certain type of badness that exhausts itself, and the nature is righted by ordinary hereditary reactions, and that is frequently mistaken for the regenerating work of God. If it is the work of the Spirit of God, repentance is its basis. We can only test the experimental working of Redemption by the fruits the New Testament has taught us to expect. "Bring forth therefore fruits worthy of your repentance" (Luke iii. 8).

REDEMPTION

THE CHRISTIAN'S GREATEST TRUST

(*a*) The Cross and the Father's Heart. *John* xii. 28; *Gal.* vi. 14.

We can understand the attributes of God in other ways, but we can only understand the Father's heart in the Cross of Christ. The Cross of Christ is not the cross of a martyr, it has become the symbol of the martyr; it is the revelation of Redemption. The Cross is the crystallized point in history where Eternity merges with Time. The cry on the cross, "My God, My God, why hast Thou forsaken Me?" is not the desolation of an isolated individual: it is the revelation of the heart of God face to face with the sin of man, and going deeper down than man's sin can ever go in unconceivable heartbreak in order that every sin-stained, hell-deserving sinner might be absolutely redeemed. If the Redemption of Christ cannot go deeper down than hell, it is not redemption at all.

It is always the tragic note that is struck when once the Spirit of God gets hold of a man. The reason we are so shallow and flippant in our presentation of the Cross is that we have never seen ourselves for one second in the light of God. When we do see ourselves in the light of God, there is only one of two refuges—suicide or the Cross of Christ. The great condemnation of much of our modern preaching is that it conveys no sense of the desperate tragedy of conviction of sin. When once the real touch of conviction of sin comes, it is hell on earth—there is no other word for it. One second of realizing ourselves in the light of God means unspeakable agony and distress; but the marvel is that when the conviction does come, there is God in the very centre of the whole thing to save us from it. That is the meaning of the Cross of Christ as experimentally applied to us. We have to face ourselves with the revelation of the Redemption, mirrored and concentrated in the Cross of Jesus Christ as it is presented in the New Testament, before we get the shallow, pious nonsense shaken out of our religious beliefs. To be saved by God's grace is not a beautifully pathetic thing; it is a desperately tragic thing.

(*b*) THE CROSS AND THE SAVIOUR'S MIND. *Matt.* xvi. 24; *Gal.* ii. 20.

The evidence that I have accepted the Cross of Christ as the revelation of Redemption is that the regenerating life of God is manifested in my mortal flesh. Immediately I accept the Cross of Christ as the revelation of Redemption I am not, I must not be, the same man, I must be another man, and I must take up my cross from my Lord. The cross is the gift of Jesus to His disciples and it can only bear one aspect: 'I am not my own.' The whole attitude of the life is that I have given up my right to myself. I live like a crucified man. Unless that crisis is reached it is perilously possible for my religious life to end as a sentimental fiasco. "I don't mind being saved from hell and receiving the Holy Spirit, but it is too much to expect me to give up my right to myself to Jesus Christ, to give up my manhood, my womanhood, all my ambitions." Jesus said, If any man will be My disciple, those are the conditions. It is that kind of thing that offended the historic disciples, and it will offend you and me. It is a slander to the Cross of Christ to say we believe in Jesus and please ourselves all the time, choosing our own way.

Our salvation is one of unspeakable freedom for heart and mind and body, but do we sufficiently brood on what it cost God to make it ours? At certain stages of Christian experience a saint has no courtesy towards God, no sense of gratitude; he is thankful for being delivered from sin, but the thought of living for Jesus, of being recklessly abandoned to Him, has not begun to dawn on him yet. When we come to the Cross we do not go through it and out the other side; we abide in the life to which the Cross is the gateway, and the characteristic of the life is that of deep profound sacrifice to God. Social service that is not based on the Cross of Christ is the cultured blasphemy of civilized life against God, because it denies that God has done anything, and puts human effort as the only way whereby the world will be redeemed.

RELATIVE REDEMPTIVE REACTIONS

An abiding snare in dealing with Christian doctrine arises from the tendency to bend the attention exclusively either to the objective or the subjective side. If we deal only with the objective, it produces the type of practical life that contradicts the creed believed in; and to deal only with the subjective side produces the moody, sickly introspective type of life, its eyes fixed on its own whiteness. The wholesome antidote to either tendency is the New Testament, which embraces both the objective and the subjective through the miracle of regeneration. Belief in the New Testament is always practical and positive, that is, it instantly manifests itself. I do not 'gull' myself into believing something has happened, it is a fact; I am not only right with God but am actually proving that I am in my life. If my faith in the Redemptive work of Christ does not react in a practical life which manifests it, the reason is a wrong temper of mind in me.

How ought life from the ascended Lord to react in me? By reaction is meant not a reaction of nerves but the essential nature of the life. The danger of dealing only with the objective side is that it blinds our minds to the fact that we have to receive something which must have a reaction, "to open their eyes, . . . that they may *receive*" (Acts xxvi. 18). That means the will of the individual is willing to receive. Not only has Jesus Christ been seen and believed in, but accepted, and the reaction in the life is as radical as the stupendous miracle that made it possible.

(*a*) Sympathies—Humanitarian or Evangelical. *Gal.* iii. 6.

If I feel sympathy with anyone because he cannot get through to God, I am slandering God; my fundamental view is not the evangelical one, but a point of view based on mere human sympathy. Trace where your sympathies arise, and be sympathetic with God, never with the soul who finds it difficult to get through to God. God is never to blame. "Remember the people." Don't! Remember the Christ Who saves you. We are not here to woo and win men to God; we are here to present the Gospel which in individual cases will mean condemnation or salvation. "Where you get the most faithful preaching, you get the most hardened sinners" (*Thos. Guthrie*). It is perilous to listen to the truth of God unless I open my will to it. We have not to rouse people's sympathies and humanitarian conceptions—'How beautiful and dignified man is!' We have rigorously to push an issue of will, and when the issue is put you find the obstruction; men resent it, and that is the barrier to God. Immediately that barrier is down God comes in like a torrent, there is nothing to keep Him back; the one thing that keeps Him back is anarchy and rebellion, the essential nature of Satan—I won't give up my right to myself; I won't yield, and God is powerless. Immediately a man removes the barriers it is as if God romped into his soul with all His almightiness, it is a flood of blessing quite overwhelming.

(*b*) STRENUOUSNESS—HOLY OR EVANGELISTIC. 2 *Cor*. vi. 1, 2.

Jesus Christ is not an individual Who died twenty centuries ago; He is God and mankind centred in His Cross. The Cross is the revelation of the deepest depth in Almighty God. What should be the reaction of that in my life? Holiness, rugged, fierce holiness in every detail of the life. That is the meaning of New Testament repentance. The only truly repentant man is the holy man, he has been made holy through the incoming of God by his willing reception of Him. Evangelistic effort must never forget the source from which it springs; it often does, and all that is presented is the objective side which has no practical outcome in the life.

(*c*) SACRIFICES—HOMELY OR EXTRAORDINARY. *Luke* xiv. 26, 27, 33.

These are extraordinary sacrifices, they cut clean across everything we believe naturally. We must have the marks in our hands and feet that are exactly like Our Lord. There must be the crucified love of grasp for myself; the crucified love of wandering in my own ways; the crucified love of the world; the wounded pride of intellect. There is no bigger word and no word made more shallow than 'surrender.' To say 'I surrender all' may be blethering sentiment, or it may be the deep passionate utterance of the life.

(*d*) STRONGHOLDS—HONEST OR EXCEPTIONAL. *Acts* xx. 24.

Actions that spring from obedience to Jesus Christ can never be explained on any other ground. This is where the 'shame' of testifying comes in. Testimony is not a hard protestation that I have done something better than others, nor is it first a means of helping others; it means that I have ventured out on God and have no one to rely upon but Him. I have staked my all in obedience to Jesus Christ in this matter, and it is sink or swim. Try and explain why you did a certain thing, if it sprang from obedience to Christ, and you find you cannot. It is not the logical working out of a principle, and that is why the other relationships of life do not see it. "If any man cometh unto Me, and hateth not his own father, and mother, . . . he cannot be My disciple." Remember, the crisis may never come to you, and instead of the claims of father or mother clashing with the commands of Jesus Christ, you may be clashing with commands of His coming to you through them. But if the crisis does arise, it must be prompt obedience to Jesus Christ at every cost.

"THE LORD GOD OMNIPOTENT REIGNETH"

To believe that the Lord God omnipotent reigneth and redeemeth is the end of all possible panic, moral, intellectual or spiritual. We say we believe God, and give the lie to it with every breath we draw. For a man to believe in the Redemption means that no crime nor terror nor anguish can discourage him, no matter where he is placed. God is not saving the world; it is done, our business is to get men and women to realize it, and we cannot do it unless we realize it ourselves.

(1) Redemptive Sanctuary. *Jer.* xvii. 12.

"What needs doing is all less than has been done. What has to be done for the world is already done in God." (*Dr. Forsyth.*) We can do nothing for the redemption of the world; we have to do in the world that which proves we believe it is redeemed; all our activities are based on that unshakable knowledge, therefore we are never distressed out of that sanctuary. God make us go a solitary way until we get there, but through one life that is there, comes all the force of the Redemption. The thing that makes our hearts fail is the profound disbelief on the part of Christian workers that God has done anything, and the wearing out of life to do what is already done. All the fuss and energy and work that goes on if we are not believing in Jesus Christ and His Redemption, has not a touch of the almighty power of God about it; it is a panic of unbelief veneered over with Christian phrases. As long as we pretend to be believers in Jesus Christ and are not, we produce humbugs, and people say, 'Do you call that Christianity?' 'There is nothing in it!'; or what is worse, we produce frauds, and the worst type of fraud is the religious fraud. The greatest type of reality is the Christian believer—one who has been totally readjusted

on the basis of his belief. When you come across a believer in Jesus, his very presence alters your outlook. It is not that you have come to someone with amazing intelligence, but that you have come into a sanctuary which is based on a real knowledge of the Redemption. When once a man really believes that the world is redeemed, his belief will manifest itself in every detail, and that is what constitutes the heroism of a believer in Jesus Christ. Our scepticism arises from the fact that we have no experimental knowledge of Redemption.

(2) REDEMPTIVE SECRET. *Phil.* iii. 13–14.

Our Christian destiny is to fulfil "the high calling of God in Christ Jesus." When a soul comes face to face with God, the eternal Redemption of the Lord Jesus is concentrated in that little microcosm of an individual life, and through the pinhole of that one life other people can see the whole landscape of God's purpose. The point is, am I realizing the Redemption in my home circle, amongst my friends, in the pecuniary circumstances I am in? It is not heroism that makes us sacrifice ourselves, but cowardice; we can't stand being considered cads for not sacrificing ourselves. That is the basis of much of the sacrifice made in the world. The believer is one who bases all on Jesus Christ's sacrifice, and is so identified with Him that he is made broken bread and poured-out wine in the hands of his Lord. "Witnesses unto Me," a satisfaction to Jesus Christ wherever we are placed. When once we get to the right centre of energy, the omnipotence of God is at work all the time.

(3) REDEMPTIVE SATISFACTION. *John* iii. 16.

We reason in this way: 'God is so loving that I know He will forgive me.' God is so holy that it is much more likely He will say I must be damned. Unless God can alter me He dare not forgive me; if He did I should have a keener sense of justice and right than He has. The realization of the nature of God's love produces in me the convulsions of repentance, and repentance fully worked out means holiness, a radical adjustment of the life. Do I know God has saved me? Have I the satisfaction of that salvation? I can easily know whether the Redemption has been made efficacious in me by the Holy Spirit by the fact that I am at one with God. The Redemption is worked out in an at-one-ment with God, in every calculation He is the One Who dominates everything.

The assurance of faith is a certainty more certain than certainty, and it always comes with an experimental knowledge of the Redemption. Belief in the Redemption is difficult because it needs surrender first. I never can believe until I have surrendered myself to God. "If any man willeth to do His will,"—what is His will? "That ye believe on Him Whom He hath sent."

THE RULING ISSUES OF REDEMPTION

John xvi. 7–15

"And He, when He is come, will convict the world in respect of sin, and of righteousness, and of judgment."

The word 'convict' means moral conviction, not logical conviction. When the Holy Spirit is come, He will convict a man with a power of moral conviction beyond the possibility of getting away from it. Whenever the Holy Spirit gets us into a corner, He never convinces our intellect; He is busy with the will which expresses itself in our intellect. It is never safe to do much introspection, but it is ruinous to do none. Introspection can never satisfy us, yet introspection is not wrong, it is right, because it is the only way we discover that we need God. It is the introspective power in us that is made alert by conviction of sin.

(*a*) The Issue regarding Sin. "Of sin, because they believe not on Me."

Note what causes you the deepest concern before God. Does social evil produce a deeper concern than the fact that people do not believe on Jesus Christ? It was not social evil that brought Jesus Christ down from heaven, it was the great primal sin of independence of God that brought God's Son to Calvary. Sin is not measured by a law or by a social standard, but by a Person. The Holy Spirit is unmistakable in His working: "and He, when He is come, will convict the world in respect of sin, . . . *because they believe not on Me.*" That is the very essence of sin. The Holy Spirit brings moral conviction on that line, and on no other. A man does not need the Holy Spirit to tell him that external sins are wrong, ordinary culture and education will do that; but it does take the Holy Spirit to convict us of sin as our Lord defined it—"*because they believe not on Me.*" Sin is not measured by a standard of moral rectitude and uprightness, but by my relationship to Jesus Christ. The point is, am I morally convinced that the only sin there is in the sight of the Holy Ghost, is disbelief in Jesus?

(*b*) THE ISSUE REGARDING RIGHTEOUSNESS. "Of righteousness, because I go to the Father."

If I am not morally convinced with regard to sin, I won't bother my head about Jesus Christ going to the Father and having all power in heaven and on earth; but once I am convicted of sin and have accepted deliverance from unbelief in Jesus, I know beyond the shadow of a doubt that Jesus Christ is the Righteous One. The wisdom of God is shown in that Jesus Christ was made unto us righteousness . . . (1 Cor. i. 30). That means that God can justly justify the unjust and remain righteous. In the Cross of Calvary Our Lord is revealed as the Just One making men just before God. God never justifies men outside Christ. No man can stand for one second on any right or justice of his own; but as he abides in Christ, Jesus Christ is made righteousness unto him (see Phil. iii. 8–9). Nowadays the tendency is to switch away from "the righteousness which is of God by faith," and to put the emphasis on doing things. You cannot do anything at all that does not become, in the rugged language of Isaiah, "as filthy rags," if it is divorced from living faith in Jesus Christ. If we have the tiniest hankering after believing we can be justified by what we have done, we are on the wrong side of the Cross. To experience the loss of my own goodness is the only way to enter into communion with God in Christ (2 Cor. v. 21)

(*c*) THE ISSUE REGARDING JUDGMENT. "Of judgment, because the prince of this world is judged."

Have I come to judgment at the foot of the Cross? Do I accept God's verdict on sin given there? What one longs to see more often is a soul shattered under the convicting blast of the Holy Ghost. It means that Jesus Christ has seen of the travail of His soul in that one, and it is one of the rarest sights. Most of us are smugly satisfied with praising Jesus Christ without ever having realized what the Cross means. We say, 'O Lord, I want to be sanctified,' and at any moment in answer to that prayer the Holy Ghost may rip and tear your conscience and stagger you dumb by conviction of sin, and the question is, will you accept God's verdict on sin on the Cross of Christ, or will you whine and compromise? The only test of spirituality is holiness, practical, living holiness, and that holiness is impossible unless the Holy Ghost has brought you to your 'last day,' and you can look back and say—'That was the day when I died right out to my right to myself, crucified with Christ.' That is the day from which many a rich young ruler and many a Mary of Bethany goes away sorrowful, with countenance fallen, for they have great possessions of self-respect, great possessions in the way of ideas as to how they want to serve God. The 'last day' is when a soul, gripped by the power and light of the Holy Ghost, sees the meaning of the Cross of Christ, and goes to death like a sentenced criminal. To every soul who has gone through that experience, there is "no more condemnation" (Rom. viii. 1).

THE CHARACTER OF REDEEMED EXPERIENCE

By Redeemed Experience is meant eternal life manifested in the fleeting moments of temporal life. What is *not* meant is the consciousness of feeling good, or the consciousness of the presence of God. If we mistake these feelings for eternal life, we shall be disillusioned sooner or later. When we are being initiated into a new experience we are conscious of it, but any sane person is much too wise to mistake consciousness of life for life itself. It is only the initial stages of new experiences which produce consciousness of themselves, and if we hug the consciousness of God's blessings and of His presence we become spiritual sentimentalists. God began to introduce us to life, and we would not go through with it.

(1) The Unique Character of this Life. *John* vi. 47.

What is eternal life? "And this is life eternal, that they might know Thee the only true God" (John xvii. 3). "Eternal" has reference to the quality of the life. Our Lord says very distinctly what eternal life is *not*—e.g. Matt. iv. 4, Luke xii. 15. Whenever Our Lord speaks of "life" He means *eternal* life, and He says, "Ye have not (this) life in yourselves" (John vi. 53). Men have natural life and intellectual life apart from Jesus Christ.

The life which Jesus Christ exhibited was eternal life, and He says—anyone who believes in Me, i.e. commits himself to Me, has that life. To commit myself to Jesus means there is nothing that is not committed. Belief is a twofold transaction—a deliberate destroying of all roads back again, and a complete surrender to Our Lord Himself. God comes in with a rush immediately a soul surrenders to the Lord Jesus Christ. The only barrier to God's love is unbelief working sentimentally, i.e. brooding around the shores of an experience which produces consciousness of itself; the life is not there.

(2) THE UPWARD CHARACTER OF THE LIFE.
John xi. 41, 42.

The upward look towards God of eternal life is an indication of the inherent nature of the life; that is, it is not attained by effort. Natural characteristics, natural virtues and natural attainments have nothing to do with the life itself. A blackguard and an upright man both commit themselves to Jesus Christ and receive eternal life; will the latter have freer access to God? No! Eternal life works the same in both. There is no respect of persons with God. The manifestation of eternal life is, however, a different matter.

(3) THE OUTWARD CHARACTER OF THE LIFE.
John iii. 16.

This verse gives the outlook man-ward of eternal life as exhibited in Our Lord. The only way to react rightly on men around is to let eternal life react through you, and if you want to know how eternal life will react you will see it in Jesus Christ. Our Lord was in no wise a hard worker; He was an intense reality. Hard workers are like midges and mosquitoes; the reality is like the mountain and the lake. Our Lord's life was one of amazing leisure, and the presentation of His life as one of rush is incorrect. The three years of public life are a manifestation of the intense reality of life (Acts x. 38). When the passion for souls obscures the passion for Jesus Christ you have the devil on your track as an angel of light. Our Lord was never in a hurry, never in a panic. "There are no dates in His fine leisure." Our Lord's life is the exhibition of eternal life in time. Eternal life in the Christian is based on redemptive certainty; he is not working to redeem men; he is a fellow worker with God among men because they are redeemed.

(4) THE DOWNWARD CHARACTER OF THIS LIFE.

2 *Cor.* v. 21.

The downward look of eternal life is manifested by Our Lord—a fearless, clear-eyed, understanding look at sin, at death, and at the devil,—that is the unmistakable characteristic of the downward look of Our Lord. The devil's counterfeit is no sin, no hell and no judgment.

THE MAGNITUDE OF REDEMPTION

1 *Thessalonians* v. 23

We cannot be deeply moved by 'nothing'; neither can we deeply move ourselves by anything we say, unless something profound has first of all entered into us. For example, it takes a great deal of realizing what the Bible reveals about Redemption to enable us to walk out into our daily lives with that astonishing strength and peace that garrisons us within and without.

(1) THE WORKING OF REDEMPTIVE SECURITY. "And the God of peace Himself sanctify you wholly,"

The working of Redemptive security in our actual practical life is the realization that 'God is my Father, I shall never think of anything He will forget—why should I worry?' When you can say that from the ground of being profoundly moved, you are astonished at the amazing security. "My peace I give unto you" (John xiv. 27). The peace of Christ is synonymous with His very nature, and the 'type' working of that peace was exhibited in Our Lord's earthly life. "The peace of God which passeth all understanding . . ." (Phil. iv. 7). The Redemption at work in my actual life means the nature of God garrisoning me round; it is *the God of peace* Who sanctifies wholly; the security is almighty. The gift of the peace of Christ on the inside; the garrison of God on the outside, then I have to see that I allow the peace of God to regulate all that I do, that is where my responsibility comes in—"and let the peace of Christ rule," i.e. arbitrate, "in your hearts," and life will be full of praise all the time.

(2) The Working of Redemptive Strength. "and may your whole spirit and soul and body . . ."

The degree in which God will work depends on me, not on God; if I refuse in any part of my being to let God work, I not only limit Him, but I begin to criticize the Redemption. The working of Redemptive strength means that "all spiritual blessings in heavenly places" are mine when I am 'at home' with God. Take up your dwelling in that word 'all,' then do some hunting through the Bible for spiritual blessings and say, 'That is mine.' If you remain on the outside and say, 'Lord, bless me with this spiritual blessing,' He cannot do it; the only result is to make you feel miserable; but get inside Christ, and all spiritual blessings in heavenly places are yours. It is not a question of experiencing them, you don't experience what is your life; you experience gifts given to your life. Experiences are always on the threshold of the life, they are never the real centre. Life is fullness of maturity, and there is no seeking for experiences. Beware of not seeing that experiences are nothing other than gateways home. "Saved and sanctified"—Paul says, 'Go on! Get into the heavenly places in Christ Jesus.' You will be so hidden with Christ that you never think of anything but Him, there will be none of the things that keep the life impoverished.

(3) The Working of Redemptive Safety. "be preserved entire, without blame . . ."

"He that dwelleth in the secret place of the Most High shall abide under the shadow of the Almighty." Dwelling under that shadow I am in the heart of Almighty God; where I dwell He manifests Himself all the time. It is an essentially natural life. When I am dwelling under the shadow of the Almighty, my life *is* the will of God; it is only through disobedience that I begin to ask what is the will of God. Any interest that would induce me away from the shadow of the Almighty is to be treated as a snare. Resolutely treat no one seriously but God. "The Lord is *my* rock, and *my* fortress, and *my* deliverer, *my* God, *my* strong rock . . . *my* shield, and the horn of *my* salvation, *my* high tower" (Ps. xviii. 2). Note the 'my's' here, and laugh at everything in the nature of misgiving for ever after!

(4) THE WORKING OF REDEMPTIVE SIGHT. "be preserved entire, without blame at the coming" (presence) "of our Lord Jesus Christ."

The working of Redemptive sight gives me the habit of an elevated mood whereby God gives the vision of Himself. "Blessed are the pure in heart," literally, 'Blessed are the God in heart,' i.e. in whom the nature of God is. God's nature in us reveals His features in our life. "Man shall not see Me and live." When I see God I have to die; when I am in God I have died, and the nature of God works through me transparently all the time. "We know that, if He shall be manifested, we shall be like Him; for we shall see Him even as He is."

The only way to maintain perception is to keep in contact with God's purpose as well as with His Person. I have to place myself in relation to facts—facts in nature and facts in grace. If I refuse to do this my perception will be wrong, no matter how right my disposition may be; but the two working together will produce a life perfectly in accordance with the life of the Son of God when He walked this earth.

"God is able to make all grace abound toward you." Have you been saying, 'I cannot expect God to do that for me'? Why cannot you? Is God Almighty impoverished by your circumstances? Is His hand shortened that it cannot save? Are your particular circumstances so peculiar, so remote from the circumstances of every son and daughter of Adam, that the Atonement and the grace of God are not sufficient for you? Immediately we ask ourselves these things, we get shaken out of our sulks into a simple trust in God. When we have the simple, childlike trust in God that Jesus exhibited, the overflowing grace of God will have no limits, and we must set no limits to it.

ACTUALLY BORN INTO REDEMPTION

John iii. 4

The abiding reality is God, and He makes known His order in the fleeting moments. Redemption partakes of God's character, therefore it is not fleeting; but we have the power and the privilege of exhibiting the Redemption in the fleeting moments of our actual life. This is the real meaning of being born from above. Civilization is based on principles which imply that the passing moment is permanent. The only permanent thing is God, and if I put anything else as permanent, I become atheistic. I must build only on God (John xiv. 6). 'Because God spoke to me once, I stick to that.' You are a fool if you do. Stick to the God Who spoke to you. He is speaking the word all the time; it is only as we are trained by obedience that we can understand Him (John vi. 63).

(1) The Standard of Actual Redemption

simply means the manifestation of the life of God in the actual fleeting moments of my life. The eternal reality of God's Redemption is there all the time, being born from above means that I am partaking in it. Nicodemus' question, "How can a man be born when he is old?" (John iii. 4), is an exhibition of cultured stupidity, which is denser than ignorant stupidity because it won't be enlightened. Immediately I ask 'how can?' I evade the 'you must.' God never debates or argues.

"We know that whosoever is born of God sinneth not" (1 John v. 18). The life of God in me does not sin (see 1 John iii. 9). If I am based on the Redemption, this standard will manifest itself in the actual moments of my life, viz. I must not sin. It is not something I set myself to do, but something I know I never can do, therefore I let God do it. "I know that in me (that is, in my flesh) dwelleth no good thing"

(Romans vii. 18). Born from above, I realize that the life of God has entered into me. God gives me 'Himself,' "The gift *of God* is eternal life" (Romans vi. 23), and 'eternal life' consciously in me is to know God (John xvii. 3). The life of God cannot commit sin, and if I will obey the life of God, which has come into me by regeneration, it will manifest itself in my mortal flesh. It is only when I disobey the life of God that I commit sin; then I must get back again into the light by confession (1 John i. 9). If I walk in the light as God is in the light, sin is not.

Actual Redemption is as positive as real Redemption. We never enter into the Kingdom of God by having our head questions answered, but only by commitment.

(2) Statement of Actual Recognition.

Christ has to unsettle the certainty of a man's pagan mind; the wind of the Spirit touches him across the fleeting moments of his life, and he gets disturbed. The need, then, is for someone sure of Christ, and sure of His Word, to patiently watch for that soul, and that kind of watching is the meaning of intercession. The Holy Spirit imparts the energy of the Redemption into human hearts by means of actual words, and it is to this that Peter refers in his Epistle: "Having been begotten again, not of corruptible seed, but of incorruptible, through the word of God . . ." (1 Peter i. 23–25). Redemption comes to the shores of our human lives in actual words. 'You must get a word from God.' 'Be sure you get the witness that this is so.' The assurance is more positive than intellectual knowledge. The Spirit of God always works with the word of God.

(3) Substance of Active Realization.

When a man is actually born from above, he knows that the Redemption is as eternal as Almighty God. The disturbance by the Spirit of God opens a man's eyes and he turns from darkness to light, from the authority of Satan unto God; then he is ready to receive the Holy Spirit Who conveys to him "forgiveness of sins, and inheritance among them which are sanctified . . ." (Acts xxvi. 18). Receiving necessitates conscious poverty (cf. Matthew xx. 22; Mark xiv. 50; John xx. 22). Receiving in its elementary and in its complete stages is described in John i. 12–13, "But as many as received Him, to them gave He power to become the sons of God even to them that believe on His name . . ." because to receive Jesus even intellectually, means that I commit myself. If I really receive Jesus Christ with my mind, I am given the right to become a son of God. The Holy Spirit makes that right an actual possession, and I receive sonship. To receive power to become a son of God means that I realize I am not a son; if I think I am a son already, I will patronize God. The At-one-ment means being made actually one with God through the Redemption of our Lord. This is to receive a Kingdom which cannot be shaken.

DIMENSIONS OF EFFECTIVE REDEMPTION

John iii. 16; *Ephesians* iii. 18–19

By 'the dimensions of effective Redemption,' understand the Redemption of God expressing itself in individual experience; but beware of limiting the Redemption to our individual experience of it.

Breadth. "For God so loved the world . . .,"

The world embraces things material and things evil, things suffering and sinning. Think how narrow and bigoted the love of God is made when it is tied up in less than His own words; we make God out to be exactly the opposite of all Jesus Christ said He was. The breadth of the love of God, the agony of that love, is expressed in one word, 'so.' If you can estimate the 'so,' you have fathomed the nature of God. Our love is defective because we will not get down low enough. We must get down lower than hell if we would touch the love of God; we will persist in living in the sixteenth storey when the love of God is at the basement. We speculate on God's love, and discourse on the magnificence of the Redemption, while all the time it has never been made effective in us.

> The love of God is broader
> Than the measures of man's mind.

—it embraces the whole world. Compare John iii. 16 with Our Lord's prayer in John xvii. Our Lord did not pray that the world might be saved, but "that the world may know that Thou hast . . . loved them." Our Lord prays for those in whom His Redemption is at work that they may live in effective contact with God—"that they may be one, even as We are one."

The same thing with regard to sin and misery. In the

Bible you never find the note of the pessimist. In the midst of the most crushing conditions there is always an extraordinary hopefulness and profound joy, because God is at the heart. The effective working of Redemption in our experience makes us leap for joy in the midst of things in which other people see nothing but disastrous calamity. When the Redemption is effectually at work it always rises to its source, viz. God.

LENGTH. "That He gave His only begotten Son . . .,"

When the supreme love of God in the giving of Himself has got hold of me, I love myself in the power of His love; that means a son of God being presented to God as a result of His effectual Redemption. ". . . bringing many sons unto glory . . ." (Heb. ii. 10). That is a gratification to God because it is the returning back to Himself of His love in expressed reality. When the Redemption is effective in me, I am a delight to God, not to myself. I am not meant for myself, I am meant for God.

DEPTH. "That whosoever believeth in Him should not perish . . .,"

The love of God rakes the very bottom of hell, and from the depths of sin and suffering brings sons and daughters to God. To introduce the idea of merit into belief, i.e. that I have done something by believing, is to annul my belief and make it blasphemous. Belief is the abandonment of all claim to desert; that is why it is so difficult to believe in Jesus. It requires the renunciation of the idea that I am someone—'I must have this thing explained to me'; 'I must be convinced first.' When the Spirit of God gets hold of me, He takes the foundation of the fictitious out of me and leaves nothing but an aching cavern for God to fill. "Blessed are the poor in spirit."

We love the lovely because it is flattering to us to do so. We love our kith and kin because it is the economy of pride to do so. God loves the un-lovely, and it broke His heart to do it. The depth of the love of God is revealed by that wonderful word, 'whosoever.' The Bible reveals God to be the Lover of His enemies (Rom. v. 6–10). We will stick to our 'rag rights,' until by God's engineering of our circumstances, every 'rag right' is blown from us and we are left with nothing; we become abject paupers, and say, 'It's all up,' and we find ourselves in heaven! We will persist in sticking to the thing that must be damned.

> **Not by wrestling, but by clinging,**
> **Shall we be most blessed.**

HEIGHT. "But have everlasting life."

The Redemption of Jesus Christ effectively at work in me puts me where He was, and where He is, and where we shall for ever be (John xvi. 23, 26; xiv. 23). It is the terrific lift by the sheer, unaided love of God into a precious oneness with Himself, if I will only let Him do it. It is not a magic-working necromantic thing, but the energy of His own life. The 'realest' thing is the love of God by means of the effective working of Redemption. On the human plane we may have love real, but low: my love, i.e. the sovereign preference of my person for another person, is in order that *my* purpose may be fulfilled; and when Jesus Christ comes into the life, it looks as if He were the dead enemy of that love. He is not; He is the dead enemy of the low-ness. When the love of God is realized by me, the sovereign preference of my person for God enables Him to manifest *His* purpose in me.

To realize the dimensions of the love of God, its breadth, and length, and depth, and height, will serve to drive home to us the reality of God's love, and the result of our belief in that love will be that no question will ever profoundly vex our minds, no sorrow overwhelm our spirits, because our heart is at rest in God, just as the heart of our Lord was at rest in His Father. This does not mean that our faith will not be tested; if it is faith, it must be tested, but, profoundly speaking, it will be supremely easy to believe in God.

A new devotional anthology

DAILY THOUGHTS FOR DISCIPLES
from Oswald Chambers

The writings of Oswald Chambers have such relevance to our own times that it comes as something of a shock to realise that he died before the end of the first world war. The key to the continued, and ever-growing, popularity of his books is surely the timelessness of their central theme—the relationship of the disciple with his Lord, and its practical outworking in the common circumstances of everyday life.

This selection of daily devotional readings, culled from his published works, presents for a new generation of readers the essence of Oswald Chambers' teaching, particularly as it speaks to the situations and problems of our day. Those who already know and love the Oswald Chambers books will find here rich reminders of the wisdom and spirituality of this remarkable man of God.